Paper fantastic

Paper Fantastic

50 creative Projects to Fold, cut, Glue, Paint & Weave

Joe Rhatigan & Rain Newcomb

LARK BOOKS

A Division of Sterling Publishing Co., Inc.
New York

Series Editor
Joe Rhatigan

Art Directors
Stacey Budge
Celia Naranjo

Photographer
Steve Mann

Cover Designer
Barbara Zaretsky

Illustrator
Orrin Lundgren

Associate Art Director
Shannon Yokeley

Art Assistant
Avery Johnson

Art Intern
Laura Gabris

Editorial Assistance
Delores Gosnell

Editorial Intern
Robin Heimer

10 9 8 7 6 5 4 3 2 1

First Edition

Published by Lark Books, a division of
Sterling Publishing Co., Inc.
387 Park Avenue South, New York, N.Y. 10016

© 2004, Lark Books

Distributed in Canada by Sterling Publishing,
c/o Canadian Manda Group, One Atlantic Ave., Suite 105
Toronto, Ontario, Canada M6K 3E7

Distributed in the U.K. by Guild of Master Craftsman Publications Ltd., Castle
Place, 166 High Street, Lewes, East Sussex, England
BN7 1XU
Tel: (+ 44) 1273 477374, Fax: (+ 44) 1273 478606, Email:
pubs@thegmcgroup.com, Web: www.gmcpublications.com

Distributed in Australia by Capricorn Link (Australia) Pty Ltd.,
P.O. Box 704, Windsor, NSW 2756 Australia

If you have questions or comments about this book, please contact:
Lark Books
67 Broadway
Asheville, NC 28801
(828) 253-0467
Manufactured in China

ISBN 1-57990-476-9

contents

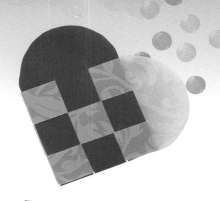

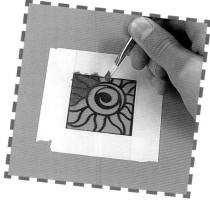

Introduction

WARNING #1:
This is NOT your ordinary paper crafting book.

Sure, you've probably been cutting, folding, gluing, and doing all sorts of other things with paper ever since your chubby little baby hands could hold on to a pair of safety scissors. But perhaps you weren't aware that paper crafts go way, way beyond cutting out paper hearts and gluing them to shoe boxes. In fact, did you know that with a little bit of glue (yes, the same stuff you liked to let dry on your fingers and then peel off), some newspaper, and a rock, you can make an awesome box that looks like you just dug it out of your garden? Or that, with only a piece of cardboard and some duct tape, you can create a way elegant purse? Or that, with the same paper you would have used to print out your report on why Godzilla is cooler than King Kong, you can make your very own enveletter? (Or is that a lettervope?) Even that report card you got with a C- in gym class can be turned into art. If you didn't know these things, it's a good thing you're reading this book.

WARNING #2:
The paper crafts in this book will challenge you, inspire you, and turn you into the creative person you always knew you could be.

Get ready for family and friends to start looking at you differently. Once you start showing off the cool things you can make from paper, family and friends will be saying things like, "You made THAT out of PAPER!? Getouttahere!" People you barely even know will be begging for one of your handcrafted gifts for their birthday. And they (and you) will never again look at paper in the same way. Fantastic!

This book is divided into six chapters and each one shows you how to make several different projects. You'll find instructions for decorating, cutting, and folding paper; origami (that's advanced folding to you); gluing and weaving paper; and paper mache. After you master the techniques in this book, use them to turn your own crafty ideas into reality.

WARNING #3:
You're about to have some serious fun.

If you still think working with paper means gluing strips of paper into loops and making a long chain (yawn), take a moment to flip through this book. The projects have been carefully selected so not a single one will be a cause for snoozing.

WARNING #4:
Turn the page NOW! We're done here.

Getting Started

Before you start working on projects, read through this section. It will tell you everything you need to know about the materials and tools you'll be using. You may have to go to a craft or art supply store to find some of these items, but we'll let you know. This section also gives you some helpful hints. Refer back to this section when you need a little help.

THE PAPER

Paper isn't just the white stuff you print your homework out on. There are tons of different kinds of paper in all sorts of different colors, designs, sizes, shapes, and textures. Explore your local art supply, craft, or even office supply stores for fun paper to use for your projects. Here is the lowdown on the types of paper used in many of the projects in this book.

Card stock or cover-weight paper

This paper is bulkier than printer paper. It feels a little like the lightweight cardboard that gift boxes are made of. It holds folds well, so it's great for making things like boxes, and, of course, it's perfect for making cards.

Printer or photocopy paper

This *is* the stuff you print your homework out on, though you can find it in a rainbow of colors. It's also known as text-weight paper.

Construction paper

If you don't know what this is, where were you in kindergarten? Construction paper is great for mosaic projects, weaving, and collage. Because it's cheap, you can use construction paper to do a trial run of your project before using the more expensive paper.

Decorative paper

This is any type of paper that has a design on it. It can be tissue paper, wrapping paper, wallpaper, or any other cool paper you find. Use it for weaving, folding, cutting, and collage projects.

Vellum

This is a thick, slightly translucent paper you can sort of see through. It holds folds and creases well and lets light show through, so it's perfect for making window hangings, covering candleholders, and decorating other lights. You can also make really fancy party invitations with it.

Origami paper

This paper is perfectly square and made specifically for traditional paper folding—but you can use it for anything. You can also buy shiny metallic foil and patterned origami paper. Sometimes it's printed on both sides for twice the fun!

From top to bottom: card stock, printer paper, construction paper, and tissue paper

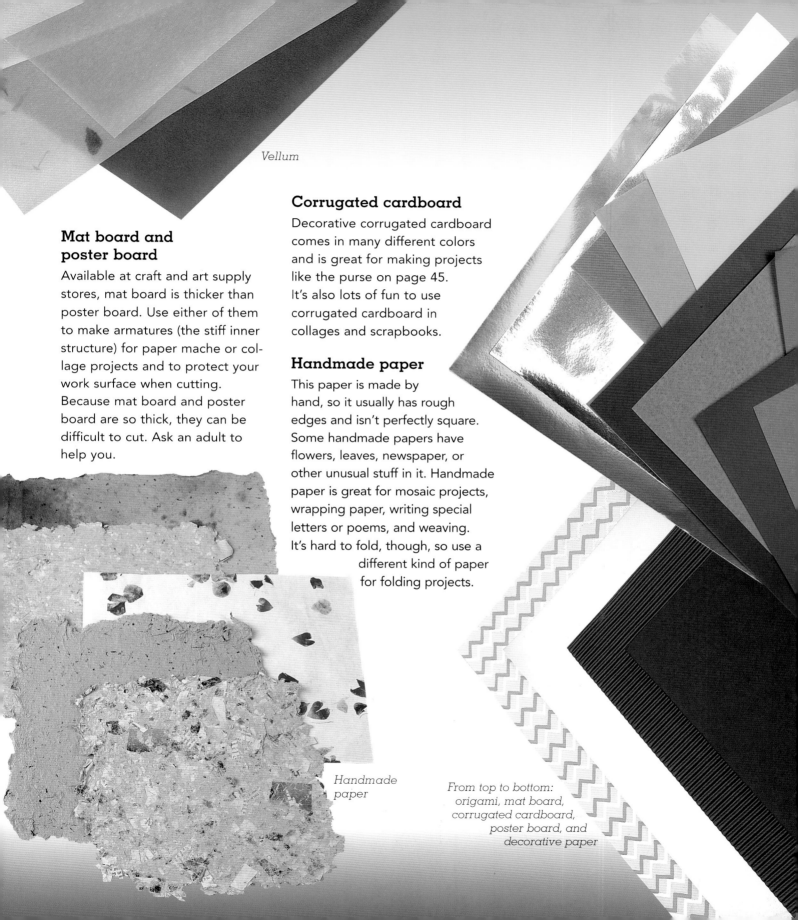

Vellum

Mat board and poster board

Available at craft and art supply stores, mat board is thicker than poster board. Use either of them to make armatures (the stiff inner structure) for paper mache or collage projects and to protect your work surface when cutting. Because mat board and poster board are so thick, they can be difficult to cut. Ask an adult to help you.

Corrugated cardboard

Decorative corrugated cardboard comes in many different colors and is great for making projects like the purse on page 45. It's also lots of fun to use corrugated cardboard in collages and scrapbooks.

Handmade paper

This paper is made by hand, so it usually has rough edges and isn't perfectly square. Some handmade papers have flowers, leaves, newspaper, or other unusual stuff in it. Handmade paper is great for mosaic projects, wrapping paper, writing special letters or poems, and weaving. It's hard to fold, though, so use a different kind of paper for folding projects.

Handmade paper

From top to bottom: origami, mat board, corrugated cardboard, poster board, and decorative paper

Pencil

This is the essential tool for all your marking and measuring needs. Make sure yours has a good eraser that will actually clean up the lines you make (instead of just smearing them around). Keep your pencil sharp so you can make light lines that are easy to erase.

Brushes

Soft-bristled brushes will help you spread glue where you need it to go. Remember to wash your brushes out with hot, soapy water as soon as you've finished using them.

Glue

White craft glue dries clear and quickly and is perfect for working with paper. You can use it to hold paper, fabric, cardboard, and small pieces of plastic, metal, and glass together. A glue stick is white craft glue in a tube. It's great for gluing pieces of paper together because the glue is easy to spread evenly over the entire surface. Rubber cement is perfect for sticking paper or fabric to paper and cardboard. Decoupage medium is useful for gluing layers of paper together, especially if you're working on a collage. You can make your own decoupage medium by mixing ⅔ cup of white craft glue with ⅓ cup of water.

Tape

Cellophane tape is the kind of tape you usually think of when you think "tape." It's clear and can be sticky on one side or both. There are lots of other types of tape. Artist's tape is opaque (not see-through) and is great for holding pieces of paper in place temporarily. It's easy to peel off without messing up the paper.

OTHER MATERIALS AND TOOLS

Here are some of the basic tools you'll need for working with paper. Many of these tools can be found around the house, and others can be purchased at craft stores or art supply stores. You can also order most of the tools and supplies mentioned here over the Internet. (See page 112 for more information.)

Metal-edged ruler

You can use a metal-edged ruler to measure and tear paper. This tool is also very helpful if you're trying to cut a straight line with a craft knife (see page 16).

Scissors

Ah…scissors—possibly the greatest tool ever invented. Many people who work with paper have a pair of scissors they use only for cutting paper. This keeps the blades sharp so that every cut looks great. Keep your favorite pair of scissors close at hand when you're working with paper and well hidden when you're not. Decorative-edged scissors create funky edges when you cut with them and come in all different styles.

Create some funky designs with decorative-edged scissors.

Craft knife

A craft knife is like a metal pencil with a blade attached to one end. Use a craft knife for cutting out shapes in the middle of a piece of paper and for cutting in tight spaces. They are very sharp, so talk to a parent about whether or not he or she should be doing the cutting on a project that needs this tool. Never leave craft knives out where pets or younger kids might find them. See page 16 for more information.

Always place a rubber cutting mat or a thick piece of cardboard underneath the paper you plan on cutting with a craft knife.

Rubber cutting mat or piece of heavy cardboard

When you use a craft knife, you'll need to put something beneath the paper you're cutting. This will make your cuts neater, keep your blades sharper, AND keep you from cutting up your work surface. (Craft knives are sharp enough to slice into wood, plastic, and countertops.) Rubber cutting mats are ideal because they "heal" themselves—your craft knife won't leave permanent slices in a rubber cutting mat. You can also use a piece of heavy cardboard.

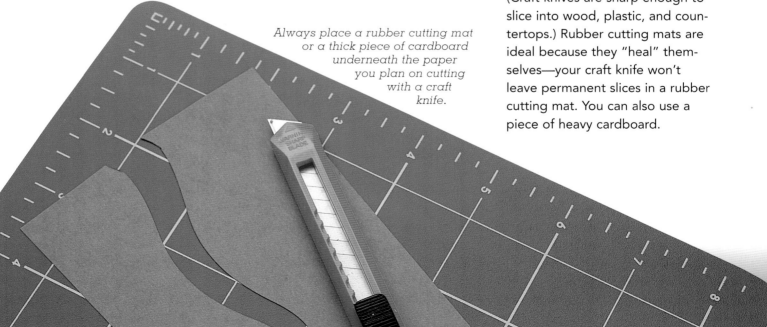

Plates, bowls, cups, and other round objects

These are great for helping you draw curved lines and circles to cut out.

Bone folder

This is a tool made for scoring and folding paper (see page 14). If you don't want to buy one, you can use a butter knife, a ballpoint pen with the ink cartridge removed, or a pair of scissors that is rounded off at the tips. (Yes, just like the ones you used in kindergarten.)

Hole punches

Hole punches are a great way to decorate paper. They come in all sorts of different styles: from a simple circle to stars, hearts, and flowers. You can use them to punch shapes out of your project, or use the punched-out shapes themselves to decorate your project.

Although you don't need one for the projects in this book, some projects will be easier to do if you have a paper cutter. If you have one, great; however, make sure you have an adult help you use it.

WORKING WITH PAPER

Sure, it may *seem* simple to fold, cut, and glue paper, and you know what? It really is! So why read about it? Well, because the more care you take with your folds and cuts, the happier you'll be with your projects. Here are some tips on how to be an expert paper manipulator.

Orienting the Paper

1 Take a piece of 8½ by 11-inch paper and put it in front of you. The 11-inch side is the length. (Remember, long=length.) The 8½-inch side is the width.

2 To fold the paper *lengthwise*, fold the paper in half so that you have a 4¼ x 11-inch sheet of paper (photos 1 and 2).

3 To fold the paper *widthwise*, fold it in half so you have an 8½ x 5½-inch sheet (photos 3 and 4).

Helpful Tip: When you're folding a piece of paper lengthwise, the length of the paper will stay the same. When you're folding a piece of paper widthwise, the width of the paper will stay the same.

Measuring Paper

1 To measure paper, use a straightedge ruler and a sharp pencil. Line up the bottom of the ruler with the bottom edge

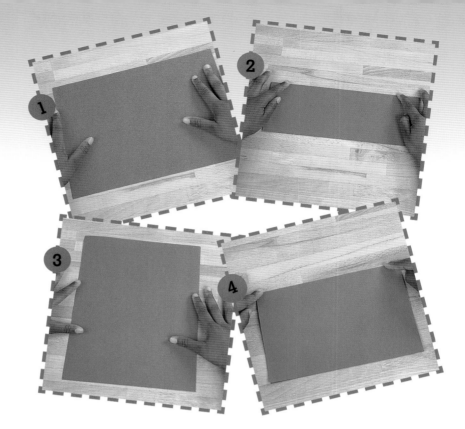

of the paper and make a light horizontal mark at the correct measurement.

2 Move the ruler to the middle of the paper and measure the distance again (photo 5).

3 After marking that distance, move the ruler to the opposite side of the paper. Measure and mark the paper again.

4 Now that you've made at least three marks (if you're cutting a really big distance, make more marks), line up the straight edge of the ruler with the marks that you've made.

5 Draw a light line along the side of the ruler (photo 6). That's your cutting line.

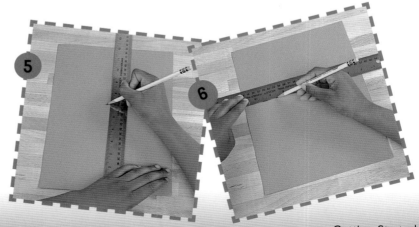

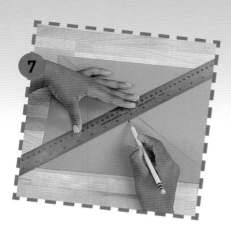

Finding the Center

1 To find the center of a square or rectangular piece of paper, line up the straight edge of the ruler with the two opposite corners. Make a light pencil mark along the ruler.

2 Move the ruler so that it lines up with the other two corners. Mark the center where the ruler crosses the first line you made (photo 7).

Folding, Scoring, and Creasing Paper

Sometimes all you need to do to fold a piece of paper is to fold it. Other times, however, a more complicated fold will take a little more work. Here's how it's done:

1 Whenever you want to make absolutely sure your fold will be perfect, use your metal ruler as a guide, and mark a line where you want the paper to fold with a few light pencil dots (photo 8).

2 Next, you'll want to *score* the line, which means you'll actually break the top fibers in the paper, making it easier to fold. You can score the line by running the pointed end of a bone folder, butter knife, or empty ball point pen along the line, using the metal ruler as a guide once again (photo 9).

3 Fold the paper along this line (photo 10). If the paper doesn't fold easily on the first try, score the line again.

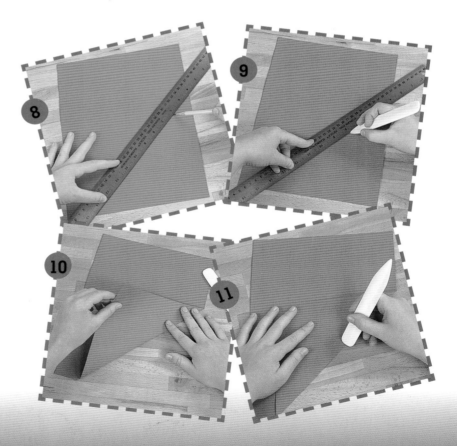

4 To *crease* the fold means to press it down so it'll hold. To do this, hold the paper down with one hand. With the other hand, work from the middle of the fold out (photo 11). You can use the bone folder or butter knife for this. If you don't have either, use your fingernail.

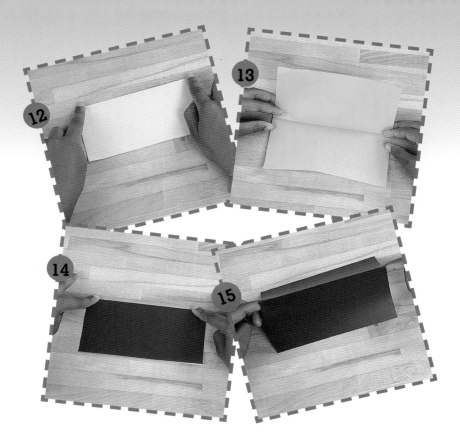

2 Start at one end and fold a section of the paper on top of itself. Flip the paper over and fold another section the same size. (photo 16)

3 Flip the paper over and fold it again. Make sure that all of your crease lines match up (photo 17).

4 Continue to fold and flip the paper until you've folded the entire length. Does it look anything like an accordion (photo 18)?

Valley Folds

Valley and mountain folds are two of the most essential folds for working with paper.

1 To make a valley fold, put your piece of paper patterned-side up in front of you.

2 Fold one half of the paper over the other half and crease the fold (photo 12).

3 Open it up. The piece of paper looks like a valley (photo 13).

Mountain Folds

1 To make a mountain fold, put your piece of paper patterned-side down in front of you.

2 Fold one half of the paper over the other half and crease the fold (photo 14).

3 Open it up and flip the paper over so it is patterned-side up. The piece of paper looks like a mountain (photo 15).

Accordion Folds

1 To make an accordion fold, put your piece of paper in front of you. (It doesn't really matter which side is up.)

Cutting with Scissors

1 When cutting paper, measure and mark the lines you want to cut.

2 Cut along the entire length of the blade, then open the scissors and move the paper toward them. This strategy will keep your cuts straight (or curved if that's what you're doing) and clean.

3 When you're cutting corners, hold the scissors still and rotate the paper to make perfectly cut corners.

Cutting with a Craft Knife

If you want to use a craft knife, make sure you get an adult to help you out.

To cut a straight line with a craft knife, follow these steps:

1 Place a rubber cutting mat or piece of cardboard on your work surface. Place the paper on top of the cutting surface, and use the metal-edged ruler as a guide.

2 Hold the craft knife firmly in one hand and press the tip of the knife into the paper.

3 Slowly drag the knife toward you to make the cut, pulling it along the length of the metal-edged ruler (photo 19).

To cut a curved line or a circle with a craft knife, follow these steps:

1 With a sharp pencil, lightly draw the shape you want to cut out.

2 Put your project on a rubber cutting mat or piece of cardboard.

3 Hold the craft knife in your hand like it's a pencil and trace over the line you just drew.

Hints:

• If you're cutting on top of a piece of scrap cardboard, make sure that you move the paper after each cut you make. If the tip of the craft knife catches in any of the little slices in the cardboard from previous cuts, your paper will tear.

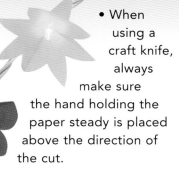

• When using a craft knife, always make sure the hand holding the paper steady is placed above the direction of the cut.

Tearing Paper

1 If you just need to tear pieces of paper that can be any size, just go ahead and start ripping.

2 If you need your pieces of torn paper to be a specific size, place the ruler on top of the paper where you want to tear it.

3 Press it down firmly with one hand and tear the paper with the other hand, starting at the top with a smooth, continuous motion.

Gluing

Here are some helpful hints on how to get the glue on your project (and not on your fingers, in your hair, or all over your workspace and supplies).

1 Cover your work surface in newspaper to keep the glue from getting on things it shouldn't.

2 Use a paintbrush, craft stick, or scrap paper to spread the glue over the base that you'll be sticking the piece of paper onto or onto the backside of the piece of paper.

3 Position the piece of paper where it goes on the project. Put it down and press the middle of it into place with your fingertips. Press the paper down in the middle and drag your fingers out to one edge. Repeat until you've smoothed over the entire piece of paper. This will remove wrinkles and air bubbles. Wash your glue brush with hot, soapy water.

A Final Note: Using Templates

Several of the projects in this book tell you to use templates. If you think your drawing abilities are far superior to ours, go ahead and ignore the templates. If you need a little help, you can do any of the following:

- Tape a piece of tracing paper over the template in the book. Trace all the lines marked on the template. Untape the template and cut it out.

- Lay a piece of tracing paper on the back of the paper you're using for your project. Make sure the chalky side of the tracing paper is facing down. Lay a copy of the template on top of the tracing paper, and trace the shape with a sharp pencil. The image will appear on the project paper.

- Take this book to a copy center. Photocopy and enlarge the template you want to use until it's the right size. Cut off the excess paper.

- Scan the template with a computer scanner, enlarge it if you need to, and print.

Once you have your template all cut out, tape it to the paper or cardboard for your project with artist's tape to hold it in place. You can either use a sharp pencil to trace around the template and then cut it out, or just cut around the template.

CHAPTER ONE

Decorating Paper

Sure, you could just dig out your box of broken, half-melted, stubby crayons and start coloring—but why not branch out and try your hand with dyes, special cutting tools, and paints?

In this chapter, you'll learn fantastic techniques for decorating on and with paper. Fold and dye tissue paper with food coloring, make a shaker-envelope with a decorative hole punch, splatter and sponge paint onto paper, collage layers of paper together, and use pictures, maps, and memorabilia to decorate a box. Use any of the techniques you learn here to make awesome variations on the rest of the projects in the book.

orizomegami clipboard

Orizomegami is the ancient Japanese art of folding and dyeing paper. After you learn the technique by making this clipboard, experiment with different ways of folding the paper before dyeing it.

What You Need

Mat board
Ruler
Scissors
Colored tissue paper
Bulldog clip
Food coloring
Cups for food coloring
Paintbrush
Paper towels and newspaper
Glue stick
Notepad

What You Do

1 Measure and cut a piece of the mat board to 10 x 14 inches.

2 Cut four pieces of the tissue paper into 6⅕ x 8-inch rectangles. You may want to cut extra rectangles to experiment with.

3 Fold a tissue rectangle diagonally. It doesn't need to be perfect (photo 1). Make an accordion fold across the triangle, making sure that the edge of each

5 Place food coloring into the cups, using a different cup for each color. Dip the paintbrush into the food coloring, and blot the excess food coloring onto a paper towel. Brush color along one edge of the folded tissue paper (photo 5).

6 Move the clip to the edge of the tissue paper you just dyed and repeat the painting process. Wash your paintbrush well before switching to a new color.

7 Remove the clip and pull the tissue paper open from the opposite corners (photo 6). Place the paper between two clean pages of newspaper and press out the excess coloring. Let it dry. Repeat steps 3 through 7 with the other pieces of tissue paper.

8 Carefully line up the edges of the pieces of dyed paper on top of the matboard. The tissue paper will overlap the outer edge of the mat board a little bit. Glue the paper to the matboard.

9 Flip the mat board over and glue the overlapping edges of the tissue paper to the back of the mat board.

10 Use the bulldog clip to attach the notepad to the top of the clipboard.

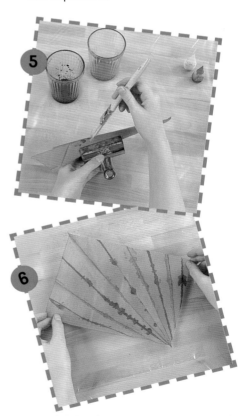

new fold is even with the previous edge (photos 2, 3, and 4).

4 Clip one side of the paper with the bulldog clip so that the folds stay tight.

Shake-It-Up Journal

When you get bored with your new journal cover, simply give it a shake or two for a brand new look.

What You Need

Journal or notebook
Ruler and pencil
Blue, yellow, and green card stock
Scissors
White vellum
Orange sewing thread
Sewing needle
Paper clips or clamps
Decorative paper punch
Black fine-tip marker
Glue stick
Waxed paper
Heavy book

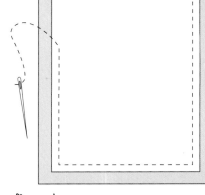

figure 1

What You Do

1 Measure the size of the journal cover. Write down the measurement so you don't forget it.

2 Cut a piece of the blue card stock 1 inch smaller all around than the size of the journal. (For instance, if the cover of your journal is 8 x 10 inches, you'll cut your blue card stock to be 6 x 8 inches.)

3 Cut a piece of the vellum ½ inch smaller than the size of the card stock you just cut. (If your blue card stock is 6 x 8 inches, you'll cut your vellum to be 5 x 7 inches.)

4 Cut a long piece of sewing thread and thread it through the needle. Double your thread and tie a double knot in the end.

5 Center the vellum on top of the card stock. Use the paper clips or clamps to hold the vellum in place while you sew the papers together. You'll have to move the clips around as you sew.

6 To sew the pages, start at one of the corners. Stick the needle through the backside of the blue card stock and the vellum. The double knot you tied in step 4 should keep the thread in place. Sew through both layers of paper, leaving one corner unstitched (figure 1).

7 With the paper punch, punch out six or seven (or more!) shapes from the yellow card stock.

8 With the marker, write your name in one of the corners of the green card stock. Cut it out. If your journal is actually a notebook for a class, you can create a green class label as well.

9 Slip the piece of card stock with your name on it and the paper punches into the pocket you've made out of the vellum and card stock. Finish stitching the corner closed.

10 Tie the end of the thread in a knot behind the blue card stock.

11 Glue the back of the blue card stock to the front of the journal. Make sure it's centered, and cover the journal with a piece of waxed paper. Put a heavy book on top of the journal and let it dry overnight.

Dream Travel Box

Planning a trip? Create this collaged box to help you gather information on your location. Just back from a most magnificent vacation? Use mementos to decorate a box of memories.

What You Need

Images from magazines, books, brochures, or the Internet
Scissors
Map of your trip location
Shoe box or other box with lid
White craft glue
Foam brush
Decoupage medium (see page 10)

What You Do

1 Cut out the images you want on the box from the materials you've gathered.

2 Glue pieces of the map to the box. You can also simply wrap the bottom of the box with the map.

3 Decorate the rest of the box as you want.

4 Cover the box and lid with a thin layer of decoupage medium to seal and protect your collage.

5 Fill your box with mementos or information that can help you get to your dream location someday.

Food Magnets

These food magnets will really stick to your ribs...um... we mean your refrigerator.

What You Need

Thin cardboard
Ruler and pencil
Small, sharp
    scissors
Templates on
    page 106
Multicolored scraps
    of paper
Decoupage medium
    (see page 10)
Small paintbrush
Towel
Round magnets with
    adhesive backs*

*Available at craft and home
    improvement stores

What You Do

1 Cut four pieces of cardboard that measure 1½ x 1½ inches. Refer to the templates on page 106. See page 17 for more information on using templates.

2 Transfer the templates onto the multicolored papers. Using the small scissors, cut out the shapes you drew with the templates, and put them aside.

3 Assemble the magnet collages one at a time, applying the pieces of paper to the cardboard pieces by brushing a small amount of glue on the back of each piece of the collage and pressing it into place. Try to keep your fingers as clean as you can while doing this. You don't want to make messy glue fingerprints on the top of your collages. It may help to keep a towel handy to wipe off any glue that may get on your fingers.

4 When all of the collages are assembled, let them dry for an hour or more before putting the self-adhesive magnets on the back.

Sponge-Painted Photo Album

Create this cool album to hold your favorite pictures from a class trip, family vacation, or any other special time in your life.

What You Need

Card stock in colors of choice
Acrylic paint
Newspaper
Small sea sponge*
Waxed paper
Dish soap
Polka-dot lightweight paper
Scissors
Ruler and pencil
Photographs
Off-white vellum
Glue stick
Hole punch
Key chain

*Available at craft stores

What You Do

1 Decide how many pages you want in your photo album, and also decide which color paint you want to match with which card stock. For this project, we used a lighter or darker shade of paint on a similar color paper. For example, light blue paint on dark blue paper and purple paint on lilac paper.

2 Lay out some newspaper on the work surface. Wet the sponge and squeeze out the water so it's just damp. Put some paint on the waxed paper and dab the sponge into the paint a few times. Practice dabbing on the newspaper until you get the feel for it.

5 Measure your photos. Cut the card stock into pieces that are 1 inch larger on each side. So, if you're using 4 x 6-inch photos, you'll need a piece of card stock that's 6 x 8 inches. Cut the vellum into pieces that are ¼ inch larger on each side. So, if you're using 4 x 6-inch photos, your vellum will be 5 x 7 inches.

6 Glue the vellum to the center of each piece of sponged card stock.

7 Center one of the photographs on the vellum. With the pencil, lightly trace a line around each of the corners. Repeat for all the pages. Glue the photo corners along the lines you traced.

8 Stack the album pages, and punch a hole through all of them in the top left-hand corner with the hole punch. Place your photos in the album, loop a key chain through the holes, and fasten it.

3 Dab the sponge on the card stock (photo 1). Repeat until you've covered the paper with sponge prints. Repeat with all the colors of paper that you want to use. Wash the sponge with dish soap before changing colors.

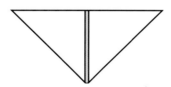

figure 1

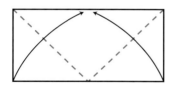

figure 2

4 While the paint's drying, make the photo corners. Cut out several pieces of 1¼-inch-long and ¾-inch-high rectangles from the polka dot paper (figure 1). Fold up two corners of each rectangle (figure 2). Set these aside.

Pretty Paper

Livening up a normal piece of paper is easy! Use any one of the techniques below to decorate your paper before you turn it into one of the projects in this book.

SPLATTERING

What You Need

Stiff-bristled paintbrush
Paint
Paper

What You Do

1 Load the paintbrush with the paint.

2 Flick it at the paper (it's all in the wrist!), scrape the bristles with a knife, or tap on the handle of the brush to splatter paint onto the paper (photo 1).

BREEZY WATERCOLOR TECHNIQUE

What You Need

Watercolors
Paper
Straw

What You Do

1 Paint some of the watercolor onto the paper (photo 2). The wetter and runnier it is, the better.

2 Blow the watercolor around on the paper with the straw (photo 3).

STAMPING

What You Need

Rubber stamp
Inkpad
Paper

What You Do

1 Press the stamp into the inkpad. Make sure all of the raised parts of the stamp are covered in ink.

2 Carefully set it on the paper where you'd like it to go. Press evenly over the back of the stamp. Pick it up (photo 4). Tah-dah!

STENCILING

What You Need

Stencil
Artist's tape
Paper
Paint and paintbrush

What You Do

1 Tape the stencil in place on the paper (photo 5).

2 Dab the paint into the outlines of the stencil with the paintbrush (photo 6). Don't paint with it—you'll push the paint underneath the stencil.

3 Let the paint dry before removing the tape and stencil (photo 7).

RUBBING

What You Need

Paper
Neat texture
Unwrapped crayon

What You Do

1. Put the paper over the neat texture (photo 8).

2. Rub the crayon all over the paper. The texture will be transferred onto the paper (photo 9).

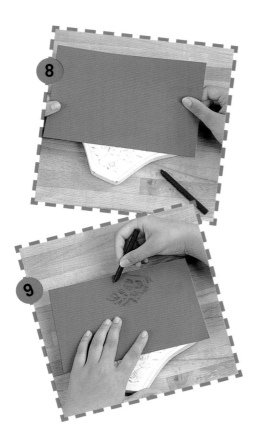

BUBBLING

What You Need

½ cup dishwashing soap
1 cup water
Food coloring
Container*
Straw
Paper

*The shape of the container will be transferred onto the page, so find a cool container!

What You Do

1. Mix the dishwashing soap, water, and food coloring together in the container. Add enough food coloring to change the color of the water.

2. Use the straw to blow bubbles in the container (photo 10).

3. Hold the paper over the bubbles, just barely touching the foam (photo 11). As the bubbles burst against the paper, they'll leave a colored imprint on it (photo 12).

4. Pull the paper off the glass and let it dry before making another bubble imprint (photo 13).

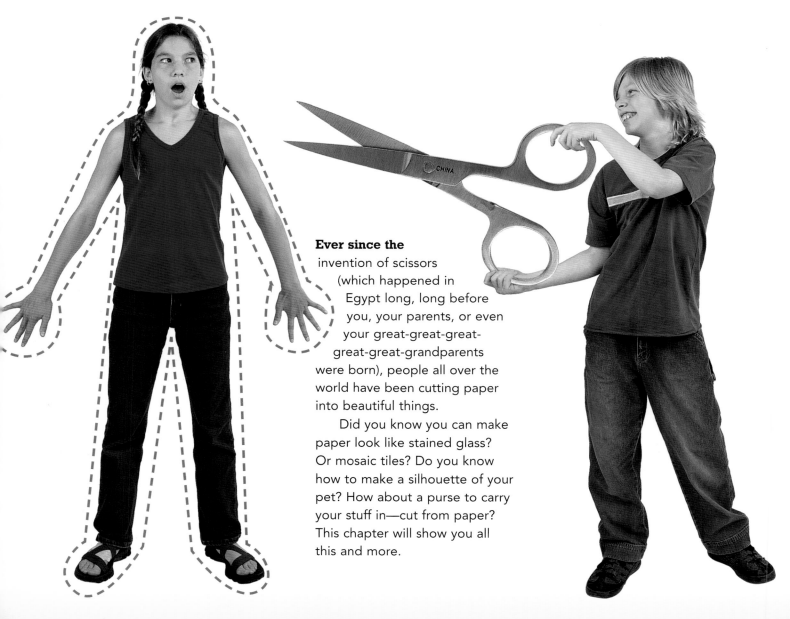

CHAPTER TWO

Cutting Paper

Ever since the invention of scissors (which happened in Egypt long, long before you, your parents, or even your great-great-great-great-great-grandparents were born), people all over the world have been cutting paper into beautiful things.

Did you know you can make paper look like stained glass? Or mosaic tiles? Do you know how to make a silhouette of your pet? How about a purse to carry your stuff in—cut from paper? This chapter will show you all this and more.

Chinese Dragon

4 Cut out the smaller window shapes in the body of the dragon.

5 Use the scissors to cut out pieces of tissue paper to fit in the windows on the dragon's body.

6 Glue the pieces of colored tissue paper to the back of each window with the glue stick.

This Chinese dragon will bring good fortune, wisdom, and generosity.

What You Need

Template on page 107
Tape
Black poster board
Craft knife (see safety tips on page 16)
Colored tissue paper
Scissors
Glue stick

What You Do

1 Photocopy the template on page 107. Enlarge or reduce it so it's the size you want. See page 17 for more information on using templates.

2 Tape the template to the back of the poster board.

3 Cut out the dragon shape with the craft knife.

Flower Lights

Make a lovely strand of flower lights to decorate your room.

What You Need

Templates on page 106
Lots of 4 x 4-inch sheets of vellum in assorted colors
Bone folder
Metal-edge ruler
Scissors
Hole punch
Mini-light strand

What You Do

1 Fold the first piece of vellum in half (photo 1). Fold it again (photo 2). Unfold the paper and place it over one of the templates on page 106.

2 Trace the template in the top left-hand square of the folded paper (photo 3).

3 Refold the paper, and cut along the line you drew in step 2 (photo 4).

4 Unfold your flower (photo 5).

5 Use the hole punch to make the center hole of each flower (photo 6). Repeat with the rest of the squares of vellum and templates.

6 Carefully remove a bulb from the mini-light strand (photo 7). Do not plug the light strand in at this point! Slip one or two flower shapes onto the base of the bulb (photo 8). Place the bulb back into the socket (photo 9). The vellum flowers will be held between the outside rim of the socket and the base of the bulb. Fill the strand with alternating flower shapes and colors.

Kirigami Gift Tags

Kirigami is the ancient art of Japanese paper cutting. In this project, you'll use kirigami to make a name tag for a gift.

What You Need

Origami paper (or any other light-weight paper)
Pencil
Film canister or another small, round object
Scissors
Marker
Thread or ribbon

What You Do

1 On the backside of the paper, trace around the film canister. Cut out the circle with the scissors.

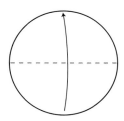

figure 1

2 Fold the circle of paper in half (figure 1).

figure 2

3 Fold it in half again (figure 2).

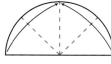

figure 3

4 Unfold the paper so that it is a semicircle. Then fold the corners into the center (figure 3).

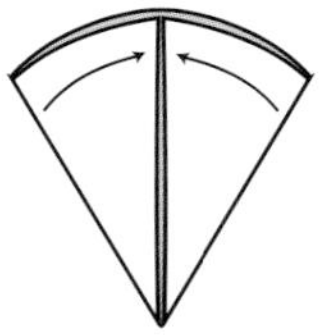

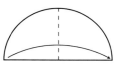

figure 4

5 Fold it in half (figure 4).

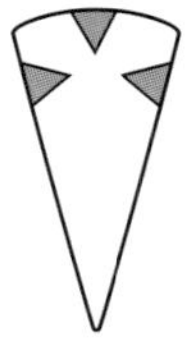

figure 5

6 Cut out the pattern shown in figure 5 or make up your own.

7 Unfold the paper and write the person's name on it with the marker.

8 Finish the gift tag by tying a piece of thread or ribbon through one of the holes. Use the thread to attach the gift tag to the present.

Mosaic Window Hanging

A mosaic is a picture made out of tiny pieces. Your brain forms the tiny pieces into a whole picture when you look at it. Let the tiny pieces of this flamingo help your brain dream of a tropical paradise.

What You Need

Template on page 108
Crayons
Several colors of tissue paper
Scissors
2 pieces of clear, self-adhesive
    shelf paper, 8½ x 10 inches each
Toothpick
Cellophane tape

What You Do

1 Copy and enlarge the template on page 108. See page 17 for more information on using templates. Use the crayons to color it in. Set the template aside.

2 Cut out small pieces of the tissue paper. Your mosaic will look better if the pieces are not all the same shape or size. Sort the cut-up tissue paper into piles according to color.

3 Put the template on your work surface. Place one piece of shelf paper, sticky side up, on top of it. Center the template under the shelf paper.

4 Peel the backing off the piece of shelf paper over the template. Leave the backing on the other piece of shelf paper and set it aside.

5 Carefully lay each piece of tissue paper onto the shelf paper, following the template. Start by filling in the outline of each piece, then fill in the middle.

6 Once all the spaces have been filled in with tissue paper and your design is complete, make sure there is no dust, hair, or dirt on the shelf paper. If there is, remove it carefully with a toothpick.

7 Peel the backing off the second piece of shelf paper. Smooth it down over the mosaic, matching up all of the corners.

8 After the shelf paper has been pressed together, use your finger to rub it from the middle to the edges. This will clean up any trapped air or wrinkles.

9 Trim around the edges of the shelf paper with the scissors to make the mosaic square. Hang it in a window with the cellophane tape.

Paper clothesline

With some decorative paper and a pair of scissors you can design your own line of clothing. Then, decorate your room with your creations.

What You Need

Templates on page 109
Cardboard
Craft knife (see safety tips on page 16)
Plain and patterned paper
Pencil
Scissors
18-gauge colored copper wire
Ruler
Wire cutters
Round-nosed pliers
Card stock
Glue stick
String
Pushpins

What You Do

1 Transfer the templates on page 109 for the clothing onto the cardboard. See page 17 for more information on using templates. Cut them out with the craft knife.

2 Put the paper for the first outfit patterned-side down on your work surface. Place the template on top it. Trace around it with the pencil.

3 Cut out the outfit with the scissors. Make as many outfits as you want.

5 Cut a second piece of wire, 6½ inches long. Make spirals on both ends of the wire for the hands (refer to figure 1).

figure 2

6 Cut a third piece of wire, 9½ inches long. Make spirals on both ends of the wire for the feet (refer to figure 1). Grasp the middle of the wire with the round-nosed pliers. Bend it down and around the nose of the pliers, making a loop. Twist the wire together just below the loop (figure 2).

wire around the arm wire once to hold the arms in place.

figure 4

8 Slip the nonspiraled end of the head wire through the loop in the feet wire. Fold about ¼ inch of the head wire up and twist it around itself (figure 4).

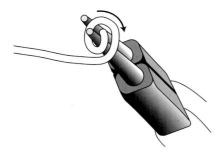

figure 1

4 To make the wire body, measure and cut a piece of wire 4½ inches long. Hold one end of the wire with the round-nosed pliers. Wrap it around the nose of the pliers to create a spiral (figure 1). This will be the head.

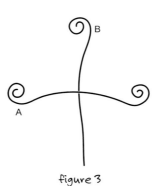

figure 3

7 To assemble the body, lay the hand wire (A) across the head wire (B), about 1¾ inches below the head spiral (figure 3). Wrap the middle of the arm wire around the head wire once. Wrap the head

9 Cut six small tabs of paper out of the card stock for each outfit, approximately ¼ x ½ inch each.

10 Put the outfit patterned-side down on your work surface. Position the wire body on top of it. Bend the arms and legs so that they're in the right position.

11 Glue the clothes to the wire bodies with the tabs. Get the tabs glued down as close to the wire as possible. Trim tabs as needed.

12 Thread the string through the spiral heads. Tie each end of the string around a pushpin. Hang your clothesline.

Pet Silhouettes

You can do this project with pictures of just about anything, although, those pets sure look cute.

What You Do

1 If you don't have a photograph of your pet in profile, see if you can take one. Once the film's processed, you can start.

2 Enlarge the photograph on a photocopy machine to the size of the silhouette you want to create.

3 Outline the profile of your pet with the pencil to define the lines (photo 1). You can outline any details you wish, such as droopy ears.

What You Need

Photograph of your pet's profile
Pencil
Artist's tape
Black paper
Craft knife (see safety tips on page 16)
Scissors
Glue
Background paper
Picture frame

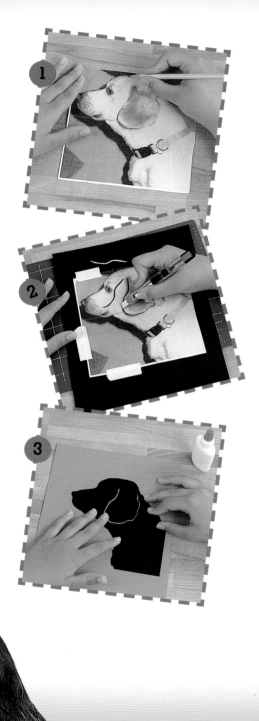

4 Tape the photocopy on top of the black paper. Carefully cut along the outline of any inside details (such as droopy ears) with the craft knife. Then, make a second cutting line just a little bit away from the first cut (photo 2). Lift up the sliver of cut paper with the tip of the craft knife. If the cut doesn't show off the ear or other detail, cut another little sliver. (You can skip this step if you wish).

5 Use the scissors to cut out the outline of your pet. For best results move the paper, not the scissors, when you turn corners. Take your time.

6 Glue the silhouette to the background paper (photo 3). Use bright colors or a neutral background. Place it in a frame.

Garland

This garland's so easy to make that you'll have plenty of energy left over afterward to party!

What You Need

Colored card stock, 8 x 14 inches
Ruler and pencil
Scissors
Glue stick or tape

What You Do

1 Fold the paper in half lengthwise.

figure 1

2 Use the ruler and pencil to lightly mark a line ½ inch in from each long edge (figure 1).

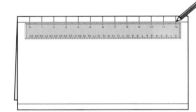

figure 2

3 Starting on the left side of the paper, place the ruler on the ½-inch mark, and create a light mark for every inch (figure 2).

figure 3

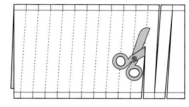

figure 4

6 Unfold, and pull gently to open. Make more for a longer garland. Use the glue stick or tape to fasten the garland pieces together.

4 Do the same thing for the right side of the paper, but place the ruler at the bottom of the page and measure and mark every inch from the edge (figure 3).

5 Cut on the marks made in steps 3 and 4, making sure to stop at the ½-inch lines (figure 4).

Holiday Heart Box

Use this box as an envelope or candy holder, or add a handle and create an ornament.

What You Need

1 piece each of red and white vellum, 3 x 8 inches each
Round object such as a cup or bowl
Ruler and pencil
Scissors

What You Do

1 Fold the vellum pieces in half widthwise so that they're 3 x 4 inches.

2 Use the round object and pencil to mark a half circle at the nonfolded end of each piece of paper. Cut out the curve.

3 Starting at the folded edge, cut two slits in each piece

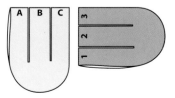

figure 1

of paper 1 inch apart and 3¼ inches long (figure 1). Lightly label the loops as shown in the illustration if you want.

figure 2

4 To weave the first row of the basket refer to figure 2. Insert loop 1 into loop C. Then insert loop B into loop 1. Then insert loop 1 into loop A.

figure 3

5 For the second row, refer to figure 3. Insert loop C into loop 2. Insert loop 2 into loop B, and loop A into loop 2.

6 For the third row, insert loop 3 into loop C, loop B into loop 3, loop 3 into loop A.

7 If you want a handle for your heart basket, cut a strip of paper from one of the leftover sheets of vellum, and glue the ends of the handle to the top of the basket on the inside.

Cardboard Purse

Transform corrugated cardboard into this ultra-cool purse.

What You Need

Template on page 109
Scissors
Pencil
Corrugated cardboard
Craft knife (see safety tips on page 16)
Duct tape
Nail or small hole punch
Cord
Large-holed beads
Hook-and-loop tape*
Paintbrush
Glue
Colored tissue paper

*This tape, one brand is Velcro, is available at craft stores and home centers.

What You Do

1 Enlarge the template on page 109 to the size you'd like the purse to be, and cut it out. See page 17 for more information on templates.

2 Trace the template onto the cardboard and cut out the shape with the craft knife.

3 Fold the edges of the purse where indicated on the template.

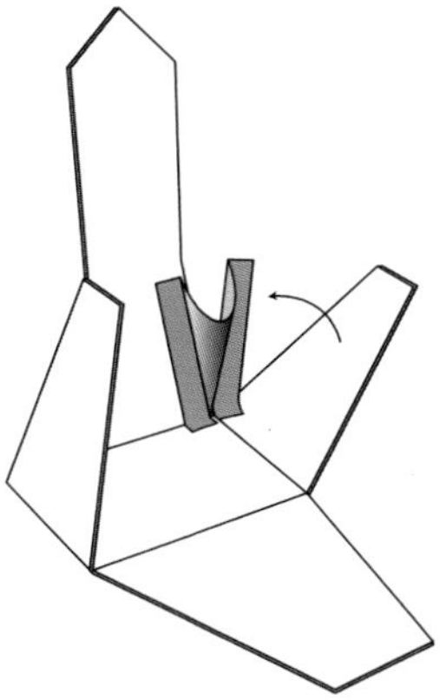

figure 1

4 Use the duct tape to attach the two sides to the back of the purse (figure 1).

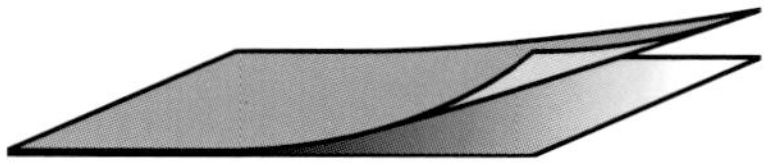

figure 2

5 Make a rectangle of duct tape "fabric" for the inside flaps of the purse. Do this by taping pieces of duct tape together into a sheet. Repeat this process until you have two sheets of duct tape with exposed sticky surfaces. Next, adhere the sticky sides face to face so that you have a solid rectangle of duct tape with no sticky side exposed (figure 2).

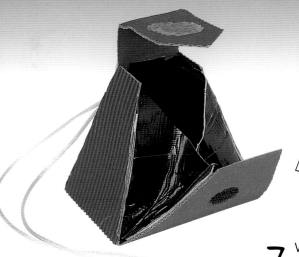

figure 4

7 With a nail or small hole punch, poke a hole in the top flap of the purse (figure 4).

8 String a piece of cord through the hole, and tie a knot to keep the cord from slipping through the hole. String the beads onto the cord and tie another knot.

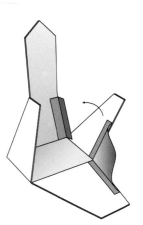

figure 3

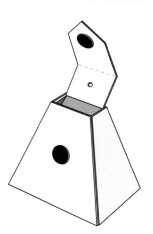

figure 5

6 Cut two triangular shapes from the duct tape and attach them with duct tape to the sides and front of the purse (figure 3).

9 Use the hook-and-loop tape to fasten the purse shut (figure 5).

10 Glue tissue paper circles onto the outside of the purse.

Place Mat

Make enough of these wild-looking place mats for your whole family.

What You Need

Ruler and pencil
Colored poster board
Scissors
Scrap cardboard
Craft knife (see safety tips on page 16)
2 pieces of plain paper
Tempera paints
Paintbrush
Scissors
Glue
Lamination paper or clear self-adhesive shelf paper (optional)

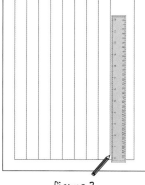

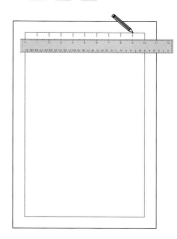

figure 1   figure 2

What You Do

1 Measure a 12 x 18-inch rectangle on the poster board, and cut it out.

2 Working on the backside of the poster board, measure and draw a 1-inch-wide border around the entire rectangle.

3 Measure and mark lines every inch along the length of the rectangle within the border (figures 1 and 2).

4 Place the poster board, face up, on top of the scrap cardboard. Carefully cut out the lines you drew in step 3 with the craft knife. Don't cut into the border going around the paper.

5 Paint patterns on both pieces of plain paper. Use contrasting colors to make a fun, abstract design and, if you want, while the paint is still wet, use the eraser end of a pencil to create a wavy line in the paint.

6 When the papers are dry, cut them lengthwise into 1-inch-wide strips.

7 Select a colored strip to begin weaving with. Weave the strip of paper over the first strip of poster board and under the next (figure 3). Continue alternating over and under until

you've finished weaving the strip. Tuck the ends under the border and glue them into place.

8 Select a contrasting colored strip of paper and continue weaving. This time, start by going under the first strip of poster board.

9 Continue this weaving pattern until there is no more room. Slide each strip up so that it fits snugly and neatly next to the previous one.

10 Make sure the ends of all the strips are tucked neatly under the border and glued in place.

11 Either bring the place mat to an office supply store to have it laminated, or laminate it yourself.

12 To laminate it, cut a piece of the lamination or shelf paper slightly larger than the place mat. Peel off the backing and place it sticky-side up onto your work surface. Carefully place the mat on the paper and smooth it down. Cut a second piece and place it on top of the place mat. Cut around the edges until the lamination or shelf paper is the same length around the mat.

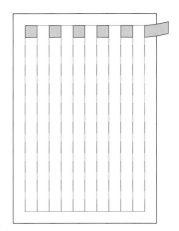

figure 3

CHAPTER THREE

Folding Paper

It's physically impossible to fold a piece of paper in half nine times in a row. (Don't believe us? Go ahead and try it.) When you're done trying, check out this chapter on folding paper. You'll learn a few of the millions of other ways to fold paper.

You'll learn to fold a bracelet, a book so small you can wear it as a necklace, a box, and more. You can fold paper to make decorations for your room, or presents for your friends. (So give up on the "in half nine times in a row" thing. We told you it's impossible!)

Paper-filled ornaments

Make sure to use lightweight papers that have color or patterns on both sides, since you'll be seeing both sides in the ornaments.

What You Need
Fancy papers, 8½ x 11 inches each
Scissors
Clear glass ball ornaments*

*Available at craft supply stores

What You Do

1 Cut one sheet of paper into thirds, so that each strip is 8½ inches long and about 3⅝ inches wide.

2 Fold one of the strips accordion-style the long way (so you'll have an accordion-folded strip that's 3⅝ inches wide). Make the folds about ¼ inch apart. Do this for all three of the strips.

3 Hold one folded strip in one hand and cut it into ¼-inch pieces. You should get about 14 strips from each piece of accordion-folded paper.

4 Follow steps 1 through 3 for each sheet of paper.

5 Pull all the folded strips open slightly. Take the tops off the ornaments, fill them with strips of paper, and put the tops back on.

Paper Bouquet

Buy lots of different
colored tissue
paper and make
all of your
favorite flowers.

What You Need

2 pieces of purple tissue paper,
   15 x 20 inches
2 pieces of yellow tissue paper,
   7½ x 20 inches
Heavy floral wire, 18 inches long
   for each flower*
Scissors

*Available at craft stores

What You Do

1 Fold all of the pieces of tissue paper in half lengthwise to mark their centers (photo 1). (This will make it easier to keep them all lined up.)

2 Stack the four pieces of tissue paper together so that the smaller pieces are on top of the larger ones. Make sure their center lines match up. Place the paper pile in front of you widthwise, and accordion fold about 1 inch apart (photo 2).

3 Fold the piece of floral wire in half, slip it around the center of the folded tissue papers, and wrap the ends of the wire together to hold the fold in place (photo 3).

4 Cut along the ends and tops of the folds on the outside edge of the purple tissue paper to make petals (photo 4).

5 Gently pull the top page out to open the flower (photo 5). Shape the petals with your fingers as you open them. Open the rest of the flower in the same way.

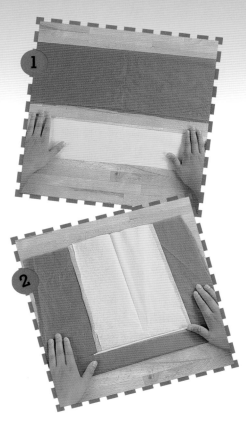

Variations

You can create different flowers by altering colors, the sizes of the sheets of tissue paper, and the petal cuts. Here are some examples:

Black-Eyed Susan: Use yellow for the petals and black for the center.

Mexican Sunflower: Use orange and red half-sheets for the petals and gold for the center.

Fantasy Flower: Use silver for the petals and black for the center.

Sunflower: Use brown for the center and make it larger so that just the outside ends of the petals show.

Red-Fringed Poppy: Use red for the petals, but don't cut them, since poppy petals aren't distinct. Make the center out of two 5 x 7½-inch sheets of black. Cut halfway to the center to make the edges look fringed.

53

Animal Print Box

This little box is the purrfect place to hide your wild things.

What You Need

Ruler and pencil
Scissors
2 pieces of 8½ x 11-inch
  animal print paper or
  lightweight card stock
Glue stick (optional)

What You Do

1 Measure and cut an 8-inch square from the animal print paper.

2 With the ruler and pencil, mark the center of the square on the backside of the paper.

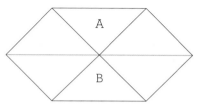

figure 1

3 Fold two corners opposite one another to the center and make nice creases (figure 1). These two corners are now triangles A and B.

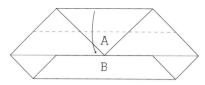

figure 2

4 Fold the two corners you just folded (A and B) into the center again (figure 2). The flat edges of the fold should meet. Crease both of the new folds well.

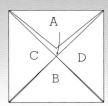

figure 3

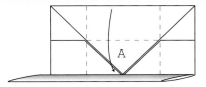

figure 6

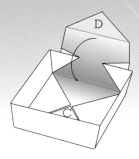

figure 8

center again so that their flat edges meet (figure 5). Crease those folds well and open them up all the way.

5 Open up the last fold you made, then fold the other two corners (triangles C and D) into the center and crease them (figure 3).

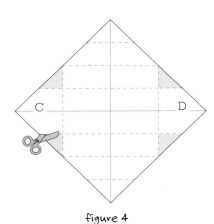

figure 4

6 Unfold the paper so that it's an 8-inch square again. Look carefully at the fold lines. Find the four small triangles formed by the fold lines (figure 4). Carefully cut them out.

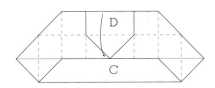

figure 5

7 Fold triangles C and D into the center. Fold them into the

8 Fold triangles A and B into the center. Fold them into the center again so that their flat edges meet. Open them up halfway, keeping the points of the triangles in the center (figure 6). These are the first two sides of the box.

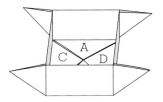

figure 7

9 Fold triangles C and D so that their points meet in the center of the box, and they're forming sides. Your box should now look like figure 7.

10 Reverse the folds of the four triangles that are making your box not look like a box. Pull triangle C up and over the reverse-folded triangles (figure 8). Repeat on the other side with triangle D.

11 For the bottom of the box, cut an 7¾-inch square from the second sheet and repeat the instructions from step 2.

3-D Birthday Greetings

Show that you care with style and flair!

What You Need

2 sheets of construction paper or
    card stock, cut to 5½ x 12 inches
Ruler and pencil
Scissors
Template on page 110
Markers

What You Do

1 Fold each piece of paper
    in half lengthwise, making
sure to match the edges. Open
the fold. Fold both ends to the
center crease.

2 Stand the two pieces of paper
    up so that one looks like a **W**
and the other an **M** (figure 1).

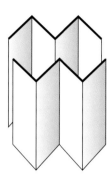

figure 1

figure 2

3 Fold up the **W**. Measure and mark a vertical line up the center of the folded **W**. From the bottom cut 2¾ inches up the line through all four layers (figure 2).

figure 3

4 Fold up the **M**. Measure and mark a vertical line down the center of the folded **M**. From the top cut 2¾ inches down the line through all four layers (figure 3).

5 Lay the **W** down on the table so there are two mountain folds pointing up. (The slits are on the bottom end.)

6 Trace or photocopy the templates on page 110. See page 17 for more information on using templates. Center the candle template on the left mountain fold ¾ inch down from the top of

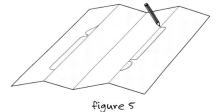

figure 4

the sheet (figure 4). Trace the candle template. Fold the paper up and cut through both layers with scissors.

figure 5

7 Trace the exclamation template on the right mountain fold ¾ inch down from the top of the sheet (figure 5). Fold and cut through both layers.

8 Take **M** and lay it down on the table so there is only one "mountain" fold. Trace the cake template on the "mountain" fold ¾ inch from the top. Cut through both layers with scissors.

9 Stand up the **M** card, and gently fit the **W** card into the **M** by lining up the slits.

10 Notice the spaces where you can color or decorate behind the cutouts. Mark these areas so you can be sure which parts to color when you take apart the card.

11 Take apart the card. Color and decorate it with the markers. Then, gently put the card back together and fold it shut.

The Amazing Enveletter

Or is it a lettervope? Either way, this two-in-one letter AND envelope is fun to send and read.

What You Need

8½ x 11-inch piece of paper
Pencil and ruler
Markers, crayons, rubber stamps,
  or other decoration

What You Do

1 Place the sheet of paper widthwise in front of you. Write a letter to a friend, parents, or a pen pal. Decorate the other side.

figure 1

2 With the pencil and ruler, lightly draw a line 2½ inches from the top left edge (figure 1).

figure 2

3 Fold the top right corner to meet the line you drew (figure 2).

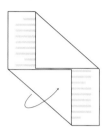

figure 3

4 Fold the lower left corner to meet the lower edge of the top fold (figure 3).

figure 4

5 Fold the bottom right corner so that it's flush with the left edge (figure 4).

figure 5

6 Fold the top down so that there's a little triangle below the fold, making sure to line up the right edges together (figure 5).

figure 6

7 Fold the tip over to the front (figure 6). Address the envelope, add a stamp, and mail.

Book Necklace

This little book is perfect for recording your observations. Make one like ours in which to draw the world around you, or create your own. Wear it around your neck and you'll always have something to write on.

What You Need

8½ x 11-inch piece of white paper
Ruler and pencil
Scissors
Manila file folder
Stapler
Thin nail
Ribbon
Colored pencils, crayons, or markers
Glue stick

What You Do

1 Measure and cut a 2¼ x 10½-inch strip from the piece of paper.

2 Measure in 1½ inches from one end of the long paper strip you just cut. Fold the strip at this point. Continue accordion folding the strip. Fold the paper neatly, and crease each fold well. Set this piece aside.

3 Measure and cut a 2 x 4½-inch rectangle from the manila file folder.

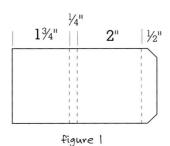

¼"

1¾"   2"   ½"

figure 1

4 Transfer the measurements shown in figure 1 onto the inside of the manila rectangle. Fold the rectangle and cut the corners as the illustration shows.

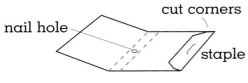

nail hole   cut corners   staple

figure 2

5 Staple once just above the short fold line (figure 2). Glue the last page of the accordion-folded booklet to the back of the folded cover. The longer front flap will tuck into the shorter one when the book is closed (like a matchbook).

6 With the nail, punch a hole in the center of the narrow spine at the top of the book (the space between the back cover and front flap) as shown in figure 2).

7 Cut a length of ribbon long enough to fit over your head. Tie the ends together. Thread the folded end of the ribbon through the hole from the inside out. The knot will catch on the inside of the book.

8 With the pencil, draw small nature images on the left-over manila file folder. Color in the images with the colored pencils, crayons, or markers and cut them out. Glue them to the cover of your book. Draw, doodle, or write to your heart's content.

Interlocking Paper Bracelet

These lovely bracelets are quite easy to make once you get the hang of how the paper pieces slip together.

What You Need

Ruler and pencil
Scissors or paper cutter
   (and adult supervision)
Recycled paper or thin
   paper of choice
Bone folder

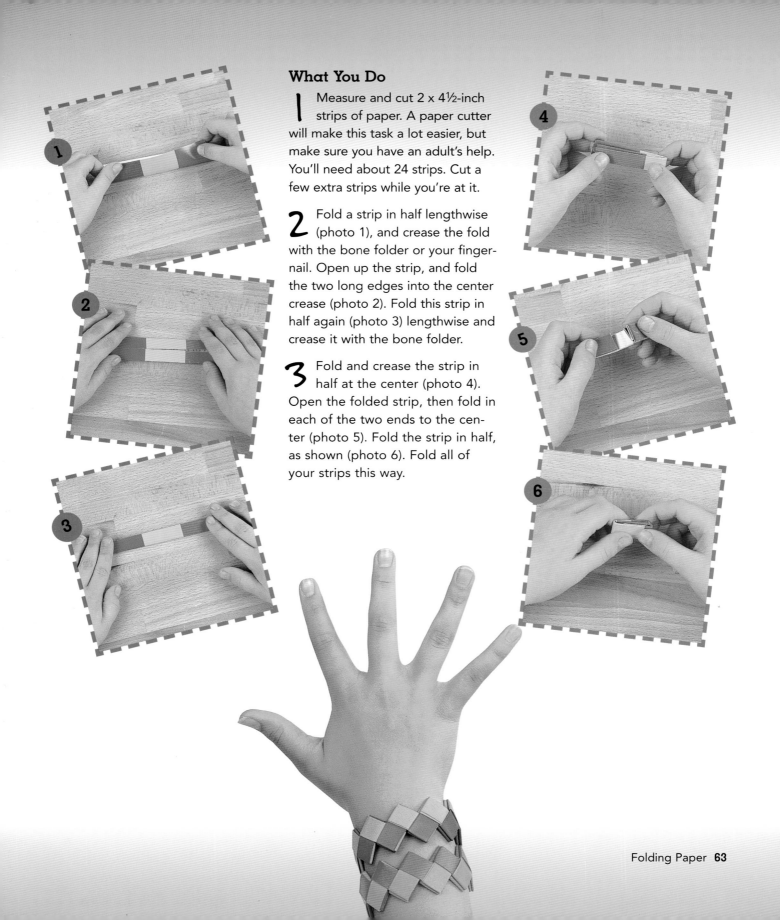

What You Do

1 Measure and cut 2 x 4½-inch strips of paper. A paper cutter will make this task a lot easier, but make sure you have an adult's help. You'll need about 24 strips. Cut a few extra strips while you're at it.

2 Fold a strip in half lengthwise (photo 1), and crease the fold with the bone folder or your fingernail. Open up the strip, and fold the two long edges into the center crease (photo 2). Fold this strip in half again (photo 3) lengthwise and crease it with the bone folder.

3 Fold and crease the strip in half at the center (photo 4). Open the folded strip, then fold in each of the two ends to the center (photo 5). Fold the strip in half, as shown (photo 6). Fold all of your strips this way.

4 Before interlocking the strips into the bracelet, take a moment to look carefully at a folded strip. You will see that one edge is a solid fold (photo 7 top) and the opposite edge is composed of two folded edges (photo 7 bottom).

5 Always look at the folded edges to determine where you're going to interlock a folded strip. The rule is to always insert your folded strips with the solid fold into the edge of the other strip made of one solid fold. Begin by interlocking two strips at right angles to one another. Pull them together snugly (photos 8 and 9).

6 Continue interlocking strips until you have made a chain the length you'll need in order to slip it over your wrist.

7 Pick up one folded slip and unfold the ends. Insert it as if it were just another strip.

8 Pull the chain together snugly. Take each end of the unfolded strip, and slip them into the strip at the end of the bracelet (photo 10). Tuck each end into the middle of the last strip on the bracelet.

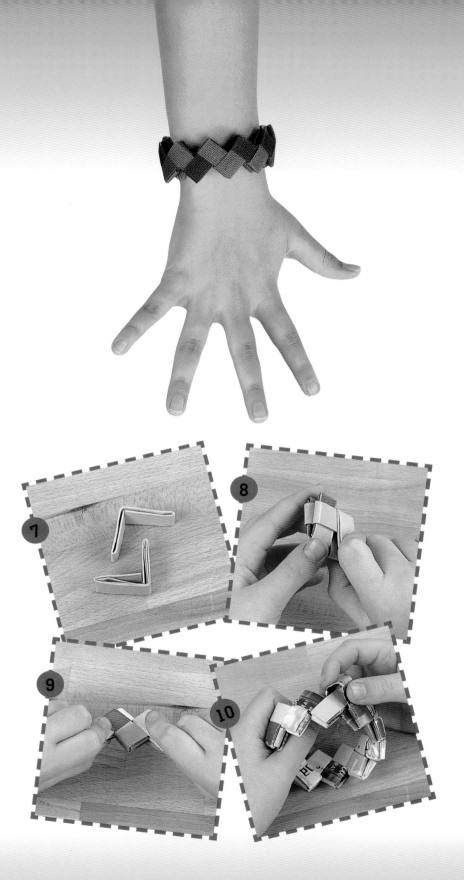

Wrinkly Gift Wrap

Add some flair to your next gift with this fun technique. Experiment with other types of paper, and create little bouquets of paper flowers.

What You Need

2 to 4 sheets of Unryu paper* or other thin paper (bigger than the box you wish to wrap)

½- to ¾-inch-wide ruler or piece of very stiff cardboard

Gift box

Cellophane tape

Glue

*Generally available at art supply stores

What You Do

1. To wrinkle the wrapping paper, wrap the Unryu paper around the ruler or stiff cardboard (photo 1).

2. When all the paper is wrapped around the ruler, push in hard from both ends to produce firm wrinkles (photo 2). Carefully unwrap the paper.

3. Wrap the gift box using the wrinkled paper and tape.

4. To make rosebuds for decorating the box, cut a 3 x 8-inch strip of paper, and wrap it around the ruler widthwise.

5. Unwrap it from the ruler and lay it down lengthwise in front of you.

6. Make two ½-inch folds from the top of the paper.

7. Roll the paper up from one end to make the rosebud (photo 3).

8. When the paper is completely rolled, pinch and twist the thinner section for the stem (photo 4). Attach the rosebuds to the center of the package with glue.

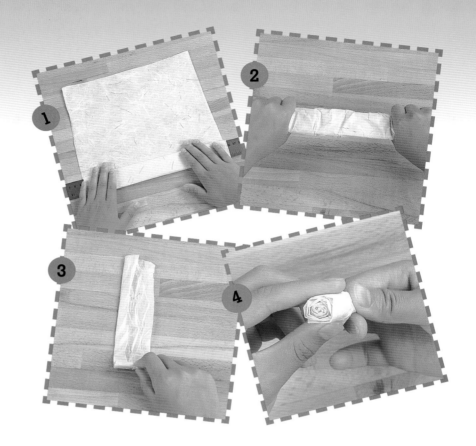

CHAPTER FOUR

origami

Origami is an ancient Japanese paper folding technique that turns a simple, square piece of paper into animals and objects. The samurai warriors used to exchange presents with beautiful origami shapes attached to them. While the first few steps of every project might seem mind-numbingly simple (so simple, in fact, that even your goldfish or little brother could do them), don't be fooled. They are simple, but like many paper projects, the more carefully you make your initial folds, the easier it will be to do the later folds. So make the first folds of every origami project absolutely perfect.

A Note on Paper:

Everybody loves shiny foil origami paper—but you won't love it if it's the first paper you use for these projects. Nonfoil paper folds much easier than foil paper, so make all your origami projects with plain paper before moving to the fancy stuff.

Bobble-Head Dog

This little guy is so cute and fun to make that you'll probably end up making many, many friends for him.

What You Need

Lightweight card stock, or origami paper 8½ x 11 inches
Ruler and pencil
Scissors

What You Do

1 Measure and cut a 6-inch square of card stock for the dog's body.

2 Mark the center on the backside of the card stock. Fold all four of the corners into the center (photo 1).

3 Fold the square in half diagonally (photo 2).

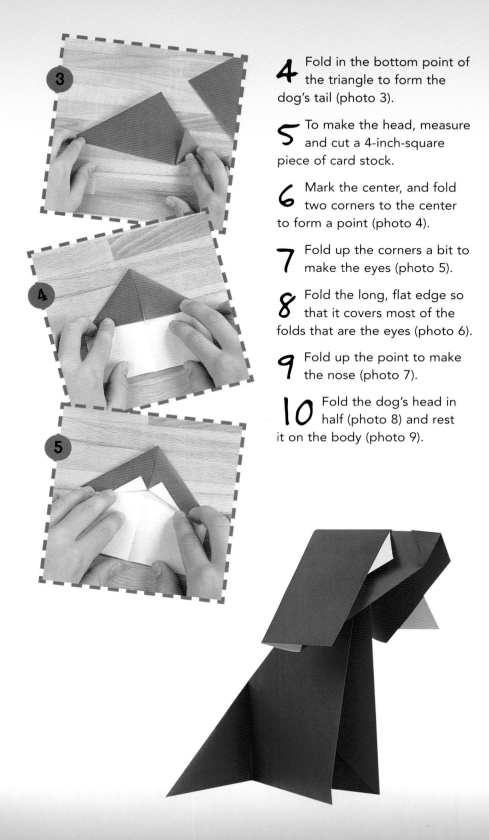

4 Fold in the bottom point of the triangle to form the dog's tail (photo 3).

5 To make the head, measure and cut a 4-inch-square piece of card stock.

6 Mark the center, and fold two corners to the center to form a point (photo 4).

7 Fold up the corners a bit to make the eyes (photo 5).

8 Fold the long, flat edge so that it covers most of the folds that are the eyes (photo 6).

9 Fold up the point to make the nose (photo 7).

10 Fold the dog's head in half (photo 8) and rest it on the body (photo 9).

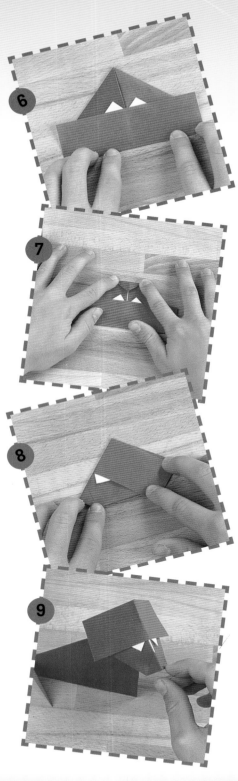

Peace Crane

In Japan, where the peace crane was first folded, people believe that if you fold 1,000 of them, you'll get a special wish.

What You Need

Square piece of origami paper

What You Do

1 This technique takes some practice, but we know you'll get the hang of it. Also, don't forget to crease all of your folds well. Ready? Put the piece of paper in front of you, patterned-side down. Fold it in half. Unfold it. Fold the paper in half the other way. Unfold it. Fold the paper in half diagonally. Unfold it. Flip the paper over so that the patterned side is up. Fold it on the other diagonal. Unfold it.

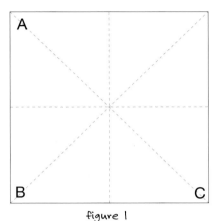

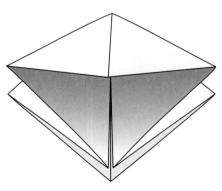

2 Put the paper patterned-side down in front of you. Find the mountain fold that runs diagonally along the paper. Move the paper so that the mountain fold is parallel to your body. Using figure 1 as a guide, fold corner A into corner B. Fold corner C into corner B. You'll end up with two squares on top of each other (photo 1).

3 Move the paper so the open end is at the bottom (photo 2 and figure 2). Insert your finger on the left side between the two square layers of paper. This will push up one of the flaps. Take that flap and fold it so that the bottom outside edge meets the centerline (photo 3). Do the same thing on the right side (photo 4).

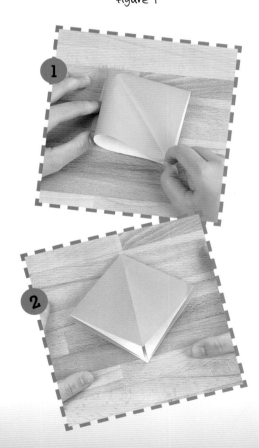

figure 1

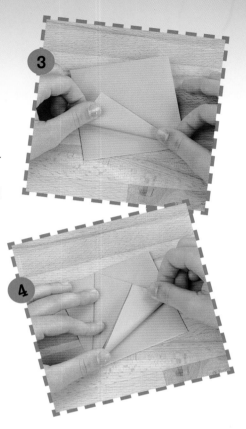

figure 2

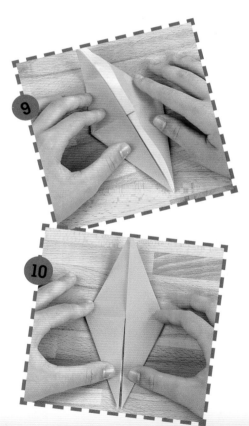

4 Flip the paper over and fold the flaps into the centerline the same way you did in step 3 (photo 5). Fold down the triangle at the top of the paper (the crane's body) so that it creases where the top of the folded flaps meet (photo 6). Flip the paper over and crease the triangle the other way. Unfold the flaps on both sides of the paper (photo 7).

5 You're now ready to form the wings of the crane. Pull the top layer of the paper up and over the triangle of the crane's body as shown in photo 8. As you do this, the edges will pull up. Fold them in so that the outside edges meet in the center, following the crease lines (photo 9).

6 Flip the paper over and repeat step 5 on the other side. Your paper is now an oblong diamond shape (photo 10).

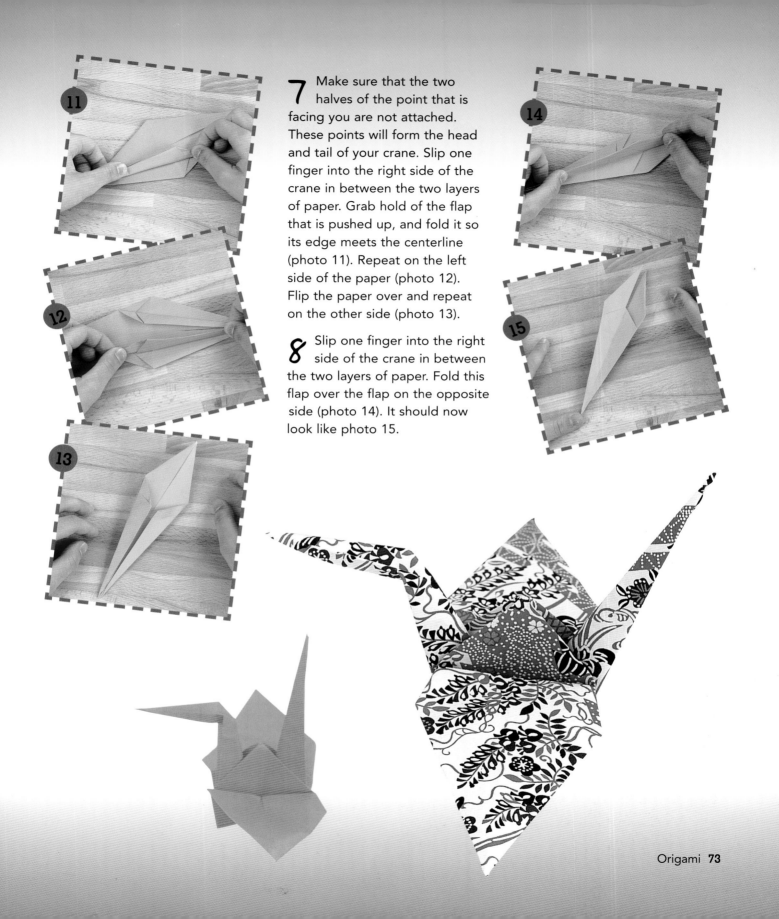

7 Make sure that the two halves of the point that is facing you are not attached. These points will form the head and tail of your crane. Slip one finger into the right side of the crane in between the two layers of paper. Grab hold of the flap that is pushed up, and fold it so its edge meets the centerline (photo 11). Repeat on the left side of the paper (photo 12). Flip the paper over and repeat on the other side (photo 13).

8 Slip one finger into the right side of the crane in between the two layers of paper. Fold this flap over the flap on the opposite side (photo 14). It should now look like photo 15.

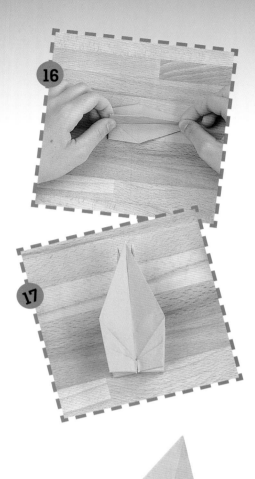

9 Pull up the point as high as it will go. Refold the left flap so that the point is sandwiched in between the sides of the crane (photo 16).

10 Fold the flap on the left over and repeat step 9 so your crane looks like photo 17.

11 Hold the base of the crane in one hand. With the other hand, fold the wing down until you can't fold it over anymore (photo 18). Flip the crane over and repeat on the other side (photo 19).

12 Pull the head and tail so they're at an angle (photo 20). To make the beak of the crane, grasp one point, just below where you want the head to start, between your thumb and forefinger. With the other hand, put your fingernail on the center crease and push it between your thumb and forefinger. Pinch the head to reinforce the crease (photo 21). Curl the tips of the wings around your finger if you want.

Crane Earrings

These adorable earrings will make your earlobes feel like they're flying away.

What You Need

2 square pieces of paper, 2 inches each
2 head pins*
Wire cutters*
Round-nosed pliers*
2 earring wires*

*Available in the jewelry section of craft supply stores

What You Do

1 Following the peace crane instructions on page 70, make two cranes with the square pieces of paper.

2 Poke one of the head pins through the hole in the bottom of the first bird and out through the peak of the body (photo 1).

3 Trim the head pin with the wire cutters so that there's about ¾ inch of wire sticking out through the top of the crane (photo1).

4 Wrap the end of the wire around one of the jaws of the round-nosed pliers. Bend it into a loop (photo 2) and trim off the excess with the wire cutters.

5 Attach the loop in the head pin to the loop in the earring wire (photo 3).

6 Repeat steps 2 through 5 to make the other earring.

Flying Crane

Once you get the hang of making the Peace Crane on page 70, this flying version is a cinch.

What You Need

Origami paper

What You Do

1 Following the instructions for the peace crane, fold the origami paper through step 6.

2 Skip step 7. Then follow steps 8 through 10.

3 Fold down the wings at an angle, so that the wings angle up toward the head.

4 Fold the beak, following step 12 from the Peace Crane instructions.

5 To make the wings of the crane flap, hold the neck and pull up the tail gently.

Super Stars

These stars are
out of this world!

What You Need
6 pieces of origami paper

What You Do

1 Put the first piece of paper in front of you, patterned-side down. Fold it in half. Unfold it and fold it in half the other way. Unfold the paper and fold it in half diagonally. Unfold it and fold it on the other diagonal. Unfold it.

2 Fold the top and bottom edges into the center (photo 1). Unfold and fold the side edges into the center (photo 2). Unfold.

3 Hold the paper patterned-side up, and locate two small squares in opposite corners. Reverse fold the two squares as shown in photo 3.

4 Hold the piece of paper at the two corners you just folded under. Push down the middle of the paper gently (photo 4).

5 Squeeze together the top edges on either side of the folded-under corners (photos 5 and 6).

6 Repeat steps 1 through 5 with the other five pieces of paper.

7 Look at the folded paper shapes carefully (photo 7). Each piece has four arms and a cross shape in the middle. Two of the arms are square on the ends; the other two have triangles.

8 To interlock the first two pieces of paper, insert a squared end of the first piece into the triangle end of the second (photo 8).

9 Slide the first segment down so that it's snug against the cross shape. Fold down the triangle into the middle of the cross in the second piece to lock it in place (photo 9).

10 Continue interlocking the sections. If you get confused as to which points interlock with which squares, hold the interlocked pieces by the cross shape. When you've interlocked all of the pieces, your star will look like a cube (photo 10).

11 Fold down each cross edge to the outside to make the points of the star (photos 11 and 12).

Picture-Perfect Frame

This origami frame is easy to make. Use it to hold pictures of your friends, poetry that you wrote, or your favorite drawing.

What You Need

4 sheets of origami paper
Glue stick
Photo or drawing

What You Do

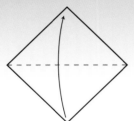

figure 1

1 Put the first piece of paper patterned-side down in front of you. Fold it in half on the diagonal and crease it well (figure 1).

figure 2

2 Turn the triangle so that the long edge is parallel to your body. Fold up the corners on the right and the left to meet the top corner. The edges of the right and left corners should meet in the center of the paper (figure 2). Crease the folds well.

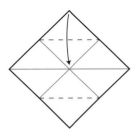

figure 3

3 Unfold the paper all the way and turn it so that the diagonal crease is parallel to your body. Fold the top and bottom corners into the center (figure 3).

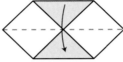

figure 4

4 Fold the paper in half along the diagonal crease (figure 4).

figure 5

5 Fold down the points on the right and the left so that their top edges meet the crease line (figure 5).

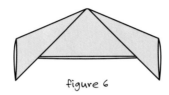

figure 6

6 Your paper should look like figure 6. Repeat steps 1 through 5 for the other three pieces of paper.

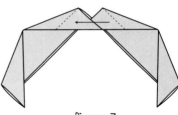

figure 7

7 To assemble the frame, slide the point of one of the pieces of paper into the point of another (figure 7). Use the glue stick to hold the papers together. Do this with all four pieces of paper.

8 Slip your photo or drawing into the pouches in the sides of the frame.

Picture-Perfect Frame: The Sequel

With the addition of a single step, you can make this square version of the Picture-Perfect Frame.

What You Need

4 pieces of origami paper
Glue stick
Photo or drawing

What You Do

1 Follow the instructions for the Picture-Perfect Frame, through step 4.

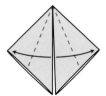

figure 1

2 Fold down the points on the right and the left so that their top edges meet at the centerline (figure 1). The points will stick out below the paper underneath.

figure 2

3 Fold the flaps back up so that their edges meet the fold line from step 2 (figure 2).

4 Repeat steps 1 through 3 for the three other pieces of paper.

figure 3

5 To assemble the frame, slide the point of one of the pieces of paper into the point of another (figure 3). Use the glue stick to hold the papers together.

6 Slip your photo or drawing into the pouches on the sides of the frame.

CHAPTER FIVE

Gluing Paper

You've made it to the gluing chapter. I hope you're not thinking, "Gluing paper? That is sooo kindergarten." Gluing paper is way beyond sticking feathers to a paper-bag tracing of your hand so that it can pass for a Thanksgiving turkey. People build furniture and even entire houses out of glued paper. We won't be doing any of that, though. (Where would you get an empty lot on which to put your paper house?)

With a little glue and some pretty pieces of paper, you can make jewelry, magnets, and a clock, or give your lunch box a makeover.

Stained Glass Candleholder

This candleholder will cast some colorful, stained-glass light on your life.

What You Need

Large glass candleholder
Brightly colored tissue paper
Scissors
Decoupage medium
  (see page 10)
Disposable foam or plastic plate
Paintbrush
Foam brush
Candle
Matches

What You Do

1 Wash and dry the candle-holder. Cut the tissue paper into a variety of shapes and sizes.

2 Put a small amount of the decoupage medium onto the disposable plate. Paint the glue onto a small area of the outside of the candleholder with the paintbrush. Work in small areas of the candleholder at a time so that the decoupage medium won't dry out before you've placed the tissue paper where you want it.

3 Pick up a piece of tissue paper and place it onto the glued area. Use the brush to spread a thin layer of glue over the tissue paper. Work carefully to avoid tearing the tissue paper. If the tissue tears, gently put it back in place and smooth out the torn area. Place some pieces side by side, and overlap others to create new colors!

4 When you've completed the first small spot, make another small area of glue and continue to cover the glass with the tissue paper. Use different sizes, shapes, and colors of tissue paper. Do not put tissue paper around the top of the candleholder.

5 Once the entire candleholder is covered, let the glue dry completely. Use the foam brush to cover the entire candleholder with one or two additional coats of decoupage medium.

6 Place a candle in the holder, light it, and turn off the lights!

Magnificent Magnets

These cool little magnets will really stick with you!

What You Need

Clear glass half-marbles*
Colorful origami paper
Pencil
Scissors
Paintbrush
Decoupage medium
   (see page 10)
Round magnets with
   adhesive backs*

*Available at craft stores

What You Do

1 Put one of the half-marbles on top of a piece of the origami paper. Move it around until you have the perfect piece of the pattern showing through.

2 Trace around the marble with the pencil. Cut out the circle.

3 Look carefully at your clear glass half-marble. Make sure it doesn't have cracks, scratches, or bubbles in it. Wash and dry the back (the flat side) of the marble.

4 With the paintbrush, apply a thin coat of the decoupage medium to the back of the marble. Press the paper (patterned-side up!) to the back of the glass. Smooth out any wrinkles or air bubbles with your fingers. Let it dry. (While it's drying, make more.)

5 When your marble is dry, carefully trim away any paper that's sticking out around the marble.

6 Paint another coat of the decoupage medium onto the back of the paper. Let it dry.

7 Stick the magnet to the back of the marble.

Paper Bead Bracelet and Necklace

You can use decorative paper, origami paper, old magazines, Sunday comics and more to make these one-of-a-kind beads.

What You Need

Colorful paper
Templates on page 110
Pencil
Scissors
Toothpick
Glue stick
Elastic cord
Sewing needle
Seed beads

What You Do

1 If you'd like, color a plain piece of paper with crayons, stamps, markers, or anything else you want. Trace the triangle-shaped templates on page 110 onto the colorful paper with the pencil (photo 1). See page 17 for more information on using templates. Cut them out.

2 Starting with the wide end of one of the triangles, roll it around the pencil (photo 2). This will break down the fibers in the paper and make it easier to do the next step.

3 Roll the triangle around the toothpick, starting with the wide base of the triangle (photo 3). Roll it up tightly, but not so tightly that you can't pull it off the toothpick.

4 Unroll the tip of the triangle about ¾ inch. Glue this end with the glue stick and reroll it (photo 4). Let the glue dry.

5 Repeat steps 2 through 4 until you've made as many beads as you need. Necklaces are usually between 16 and 20 inches long, and bracelets are between 5½ and 7 inches.

6 Thread the elastic cord through the sewing needle. Make sure the needle is small enough to fit through all of the holes in your beads.

7 String the necklace, alternating the paper beads with the seed beads. Tie the ends of the elastic in a knot. Repeat steps 6 and 7 for the bracelet.

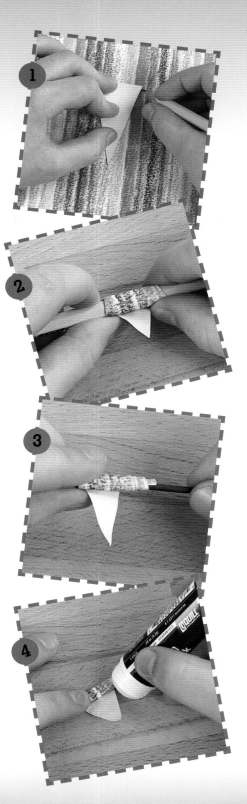

Butterfly Wings

Be the hit of the costume party with this easy-to-make set of wings. You can make these wings just about any size you want.

What You Need

Refrigerator box or other large
    cardboard box
Marker
Wing template on page 110
Craft knife (see safety tips on
    page 16)
Old newspaper
White acrylic craft paint
Paintbrushes
Scissors
Colored tissue paper
Decoupage medium
    (see page 10)
Colored paper
Glue stick
A helper
Ribbon

What You Do

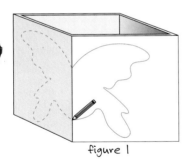

figure 1

1 Turn the box so that one of
the corners is facing you.
This corner will be the middle of
the wings. Using the marker,
draw one wing onto the side of
the box (figure 1). Use the wing
template on page 110 as a guide.
See page 17 for more information
on using templates.

2 Cut out the wing with the
craft knife and an adult's
help. Cut up to but not into the
corner of the box.

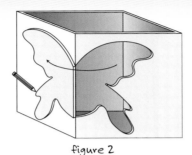

figure 2

3 Fold the wing over so that it's
on top of the other side of
the box. Trace around it with the
marker and cut it out. Cut through
the corner of the box to detach
the wings (figure 2).

4 Cover your work surface with
old newspapers. Put the wings
on top of them. Paint the wings
with the white acrylic paint. Let the
paint dry, then flip the wings over
and paint the other side.

5 Cut different shapes out of
the colored tissue paper.
Make two of each shape in order
to create a symmetrical design.

6 Position the shapes of colored
tissue paper on each wing.
Overlapping the tissue paper
will create fun new colors.
When you're happy with the
arrangement, move the tissue
paper aside. Brush the decoupage
medium onto the cardboard
where the tissue paper will go.
Reposition the tissue paper on
top of the glue, smooth out the
wrinkles and air bubbles with your
fingertips, and brush more glue
on top of the tissue paper. Glue
all the tissue paper shapes to the
cardboard. Let it dry.

7 Cut different shapes out of
the colored paper. Arrange
and glue them on top of the
tissue paper with the glue stick.
Let the glue dry.

8 When the glue on the wings
is completely dry, flip the
wings over and decorate the
other side.

9 To finish the edges of the
wings, cut enough 2-inch
strips of tissue paper to wrap
all the way around the edges
of the wings. Brush a small
section of decoupage medium
along the raw edge of the wing
and about 1 inch over on each
side. Fold the tissue paper around
the edge of the wing and shape
it to the curves with your fingers.
Continue working in small
sections until you've worked
your way around the entire
edge. Brush more glue on top
of the tissue paper. Let it dry.

10 Get someone to help you figure out where the holes in the wings need to be placed. Have your helper hold the wings against your back and mark two holes (one above the other) on each wing. Your shoulder should fit between the two holes. Punch out the holes with the scissors or the craft knife.

11 Thread a piece of the ribbon through each set of holes. Slip them onto your shoulders and have your helper tie the ends of the ribbon together.

Floral Box Lid clock

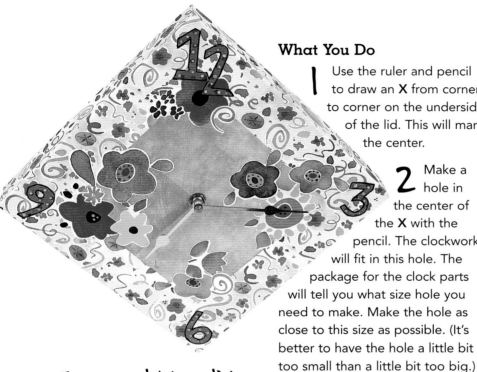

Turn an old box lid into this pretty clock with decorative scrapbooking paper.

What You Need

Ruler and pencil
Box lid
Printed scrapbooking paper*
Scissors
Glue
Plain piece of colored paper
Clock mechanism*

*Available at craft stores

What You Do

1 Use the ruler and pencil to draw an **X** from corner to corner on the underside of the lid. This will mark the center.

2 Make a hole in the center of the **X** with the pencil. The clockworks will fit in this hole. The package for the clock parts will tell you what size hole you need to make. Make the hole as close to this size as possible. (It's better to have the hole a little bit too small than a little bit too big.)

3 Cover the box lid with the scrapbooking paper to create a background for the clock face. Wrap the paper around the sides of the box lid and cut the corners to fit, just like you're wrapping a present. Glue the paper into place with the glue stick. Smooth out any wrinkles or air bubbles with your fingers and let it dry.

4 Cut a square piece of the plain paper and glue it to the center of the lid.

5 Cut out some of your favorite images from the remaining printed papers. Arrange them on the lid until you've got everything where you want it. Glue some of them over the edges of the plain paper square in the center of the lid. Then glue the pieces to the lid.

6 Use the scissors to cut the paper away from the hole in the center of the lid.

7 Cut numbers for the clock out of the decorative paper. You can do this freehand, or use a pencil to draw them lightly on the paper before cutting them out. We marked only 12, 3, 6, and 9 o'clock. If you want every hour of the day marked, make numbers for each hour. Glue the numbers in place.

8 Follow the manufacturer's instructions to install the clockworks. Add a battery, set the time, and hang your new clock.

Candy Wrapper Lunch Box

Lunch boxes aren't just for lunch anymore. This is a great place to store pictures of friends, pens and pencils, and yes, even all that unwrapped candy.

What You Need

Metal or plastic lunch box
Assortment of colorful candy
   wrappers
Scissors
   Old newspaper
      Decoupage medium
         (see page 10)
         Stiff paintbrush

What You Do

1 Make sure your lunch box is clean. Smooth out all your candy wrappers, and cut them in half or in strips.

2 Spread old newspaper over your work surface. (This will get a little messy.) Open the lunch box and pick a side to start with. If you want, you can plan your candy wrapper design, or simply go with the flow.

3 With the paintbrush, apply the decoupage medium to the backs of the candy wrapper strips, and press them onto the sides of the lunch box. If needed, let the wrapper fold over the top and into the lunch box. Smooth out the wrappers with your fingers.

4 Keep applying strips all the way around the side of the lunch box. When working around the handle or latches, trim the wrappers with the scissors before applying the glue to the back. Don't worry too much about bumps and folds in the wrappers. When you apply the coating of glue to the top, it will look great.

5 When you're done with the sides, apply a thin layer of decoupage medium with the paintbrush over all the wrappers. Make sure the glue is smooth and not too thick. When you first start applying the glue it will look cloudy, but don't worry—it will dry shiny and clear.

6 Once the glue is completely dry, repeat steps 3 and 5 for the front and back.

7 When applying wrappers to rounded corners, cut snips into the paper at angles, and overlap the paper to cover the corner (figure 1). When you're done, let the lunch box dry for a few days before using.

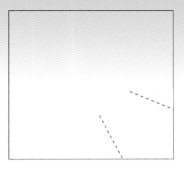

figure 1

CHAPTER SIX
Paper Mache

If you want to be fancy, you can call it papier maché instead of paper mache. That's French for "good goopey fun"! (Well, actually it means something more like "chewed paper.")

Paper mache is a method of gluing that makes paper really strong. It's great for making masks and other sculptural things. After it's dried, you can decorate the surface with paint, markers, fake jewels, feathers, and anything else you can imagine. Traditionally, people use newspaper for paper mache projects, but we've also included some awesome projects using tissue paper.

If you're one of those people who really doesn't like to get messy, wear a pair of rubber gloves when doing these projects. You'll stay clean. And if you do get mussed— c'est la vie! (Such is life!)

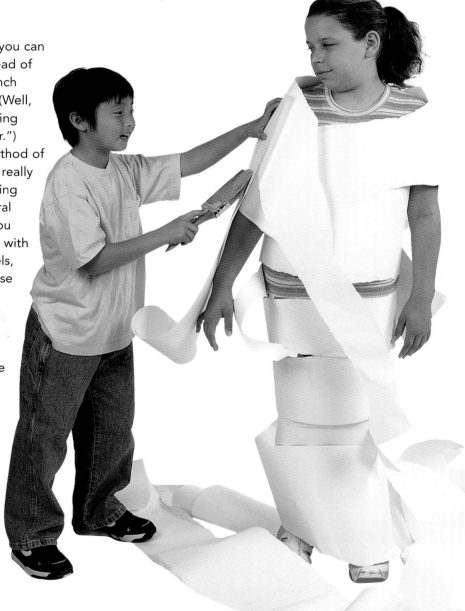

Monster Mask

Have an eerily ghoulish time scaring friends and family with this spooky mask.

What You Need

1 cup flour
3 cups water
Saucepan
Stove top (and an adult's help)
Wooden spoon
Aluminum foil
Cereal bowl
Newspaper
Scissors
Tempera paint and paintbrush
Elastic cord
Nail

What You Do

1 Mix the flour and the water in the saucepan, making a smooth paste. Put it on the stove-top and heat it until the mixture boils. Stir it the entire time.

2 After the paste has come to a boil, turn down the heat and let the mixture simmer until it thickens. Turn off the stove and let the paste cool.

3 Fold one yard of aluminum foil in thirds so that you have a square piece (photo 1).

4 Delicately mold the foil to your own face to get the basic size of your head and fea-tures. Lay the foil face up on top of the bowl (photo 2).

5 Use your fingers to further shape the foil face (photo 3). Don't crunch it down too tightly. It's okay if there are air spaces.

6 Use other pieces of foil to add to the nose (photo 4). At this point, the foil is not glued or attached so you need to be really careful not to slide things out of place. Create a horn with a piece of foil.

7 Tear (don't cut it!) the news-paper into small pieces in a variety of shapes and sizes, such as 1 x 1 inches, 1 x 2 inches, etc.

8 With one hand, hold the horn in place in the middle of the forehead. With the other hand, take a piece of the newspaper, dip it in the paper mache paste, covering both sides, and place it at the base of the horn where it meets the mask (photo 5). Keep adding newspaper pieces until the horn can stand on the fore-head by itself.

9 Paper mache the rest of the mask. Don't forget to leave holes for the eyes. Let the first layer dry.

10 Continue to build up layers of paper mache, until you have at least three layers of newspaper on the mask. Let each layer dry before building another one on top of it.

11 Once the third layer has dried, smear some of the remaining paper mache mixture over the mask with your fingers to make it stronger.

12 Once your mask is dry and hardened, carefully remove the foil and throw it away. Use the scissors to trim around the mask, creating a smooth edge.

13 Paint your mask using whatever colors you choose. First paint a base coat and then add other layers of paint to get shadows and details (such as fangs or warts).

14 Cut a piece of the elastic cord long enough to fit around your head. With the nail, poke a hole about ¼ inch in from the sides of the mask just below the eyeholes. Thread one end of the elastic through the first hole and tie it in a knot. Do the same on the other side.

Princess Mask

Disguise yourself as an enchanting princess!

What You Need

Template on page 111
Scissors
Balloon
Permanent marker
Paper mache paste (see pages 95 and 96)
Old newspaper
Cereal bowl
Lavender, purple, and black acrylic paint
Paintbrush
White craft glue
Sequins, feathers, and fake jewels
Elastic cord
Nail

What You Do

1 Photocopy the template on page 111, and enlarge it so that it fits your face. See page 17 for more information on using templates. Use the scissors to cut around the outline of the mask. Cut out the eyeholes too.

2 Blow up the balloon so that it's about the size of your head and tie it off. Use the permanent marker to trace the template onto the balloon. Make the paper mache paste.

3 Tear the newspaper into small strips (approximately 1 x 2 inches) and into 1-inch squares.

4 Place the balloon in the small bowl so it won't roll away once you start working on it. One at a time, dip the paper strips into the paper mache mixture and crisscross them along the bridge of the nose (photo 1). Use your fingers to smooth out any bumps or air bubbles (photo 2).

5 Fill the outline of the mask with one complete layer of paper mache and let it dry (photo 3). (You may have to let it dry overnight.)

6 Continue to build up layers of paper mache, until you have at least three layers of newspaper on the mask. Once the third layer has dried, smear some of the remaining paper mache mixture over the mask with your fingers to make it stronger. Let it dry for two days.

7 Once the mask is completely dry, pop the balloon and pull the balloon pieces out of the mask. Use the scissors to trim around the edges of the mask. Do your best to remove any sharp, rough edges from the mask.

8 Paint the mask with the lavender paint. Once the paint is dry, outline the eyes with the purple paint. Paint small triangles on the points at the bottom of the mask. Carefully brush black paint around the very edge of the eyeholes.

9 Once the paint is dry, use the glue to stick sequins, feathers, jewels, and other decorations to your mask.

10 Cut a piece of the elastic cord long enough to fit around your head. With the nail, poke a hole about ¼ inch in from the sides of the mask just below the eyeholes. Thread one end of the elastic through the first hole and tie it in a knot. Do the same on the other side.

Rock Box

This rock box rocks. Really.

What You Need

Paper mache paste (see pages 95 and 96)
Scissors
Old newspaper
Rock
Petroleum jelly
Glass or plastic container for water

Black and white acrylic paint
Paintbrush
Old toothbrush
Craft knife (see safety tips on page 16)
Butter knife
Black tissue paper

What You Do

1 Prepare the paper mache paste and let it cool.

2 Cut strips of newspaper and place them into a pile.

3 Tear round pieces of newspaper and place them in a separate pile.

4 Cover the rock with a thick layer of petroleum jelly (photo 1).

5 Fill the plastic container with water. Dip a piece of torn newspaper into the water and place it on the rock. Cover the surface of the rock, making sure to overlap the newspaper (photo 2).

6 Brush the entire surface with the paste. Cover the rock with a layer of newspaper strips, dipping each strip into the paste before applying it to the surface (photo 3).

7 Continue to layer, alternating between strips and round pieces, until you have applied about 20 layers. Let the rock dry completely. This may take a couple of days.

8 Mix the black and white paint until you get a medium gray. Paint the entire surface of the rock with the gray paint. Let the rock dry and clean the brush.

9 Add more black to your gray paint until you reach a darker gray color. Brush the darker gray color into any grooves and crevices on the rock.

10 Dip the toothbrush into white paint and spatter white specks onto the rock. Repeat the spattering technique with black paint. Let the rock dry.

11 Using a craft knife, cut around the rock so you'll have a top and a bottom. Use a butter knife to gently pry the edges of the newspaper from the rock. Pull one half of the rock box from the rock. Remove the second half.

12 Wipe as much petroleum jelly from the inside of the box as possible, and press black tissue paper into the inside of the box. Trim off any excess around the edges.

My Pet Pig

Who says you can't have your very own pet pig!?

What You Need

Plastic trash bags
Templates on page 111
Scissors
Cardboard box
Pencil
Craft knife (see safety tips on page 16)
Wire clothes hanger
Wire cutters

Broom handle
Duct tape
Glue
Heavy books
Old newspaper
Paper mache paste (see pages 95 and 96)
Pink acrylic paint
Paintbrush
Black permanent marker

What You Do

1 Cover your work space with the plastic trash bags. Photocopy and enlarge the templates on page 111. See page

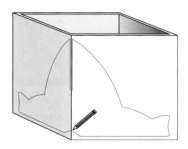

figure 1

17 for more information on using templates

2 Cut out the templates and trace the body onto the cardboard twice. Line up the dashed line of the leg sections on the corner of the cardboard box (figure 1).

3 With the craft knife, cut out each of the two pig sections.

4 Cut off a piece of the coat hanger to make the pig's tail. Twist the wire around the broom handle. Slide it off and play with the shape until you have the perfect tail for your pig.

5 Tape the tail onto one side of the body with duct tape. Cover the surface of the body with glue. Press the second half of the body on top of it. Stack the heavy books on top of the pig's body to keep it flat while it dries.

6 Meanwhile, cut the newspapers into strips, make the paper mache paste, and let it cool.

7 After the glue on the pig's body has dried, dip a newspaper strip into the paste. Smooth the strip onto the surface of the pig's body. Work randomly, overlapping the strips, until both sides are covered. Don't cover up the slits where the legs fit.

8 Slip the front and back leg sections into the slits with their folds facing the front of the pig. Set your pig on the table and make sure it sits comfortably.

9 Paper mache the legs, paying special attention to where the legs join the body. Paper mache along the length of these joints so that the slits are completely hidden.

10 Using very thin strips of paper, paper mache the tail of the pig. The paper may bunch a little bit as you wrap it. Let your pig dry overnight.

11 When the pig is dry, paint it pink. Use the marker to draw the eyes, mouth, and outline of the ears on the head of the pig.

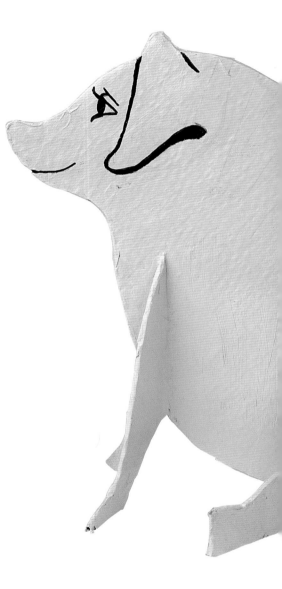

Tissue Paper Bowl

Great for trinkets,
treats, and treasures!

What you Need

Soup bowl
Plastic grocery bag
Colored tissue paper
Glue
Paintbrush
Scissors

What You Do

1 Cover the soup bowl with the plastic bag and tie a knot underneath (photo 1). Set the bowl facedown on a smaller object so that its edges don't touch the table.

2 Lay a large square of tissue paper over the bowl. Brush it with glue and mold it to the shape of the bowl (photo 2). Place a second square of tissue paper over the first, and mold it to the bowl (photo 3).

3 Repeat this step four or five more times (photo 4), rotating the squares slightly with each additional layer. Make sure that the edges of the bowl are covered. Brush the glue slightly past the edge of the bowl.

4 Cut petal-shaped strips of tissue paper. Glue them down one at a time so that they make a flower pattern (photo 5).

5 Cut and glue additional decorative shapes like circles or diamonds out of the tissue paper (photo 6). Let the bowl dry overnight.

6 Gently remove the tissue bowl from the mold by pulling up on the edges of the plastic bag. Trim around the edge of the bowl with scissors. Set the bowl upside down until it's completely dry.

Templates

Food Magnets, page 24

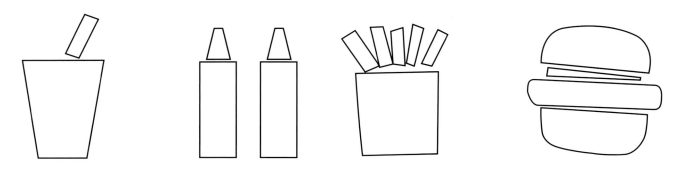

Flower Lights, page 32

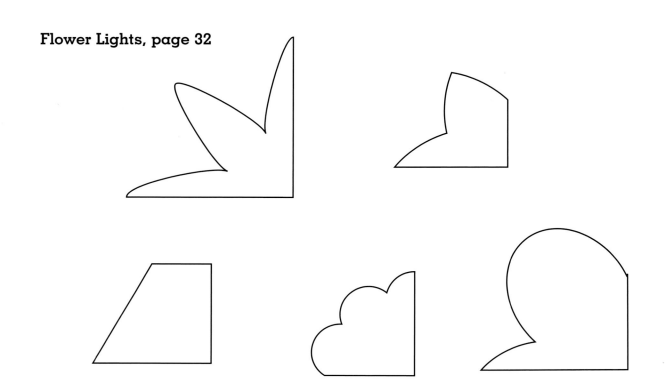

Chinese Dragon, page 31

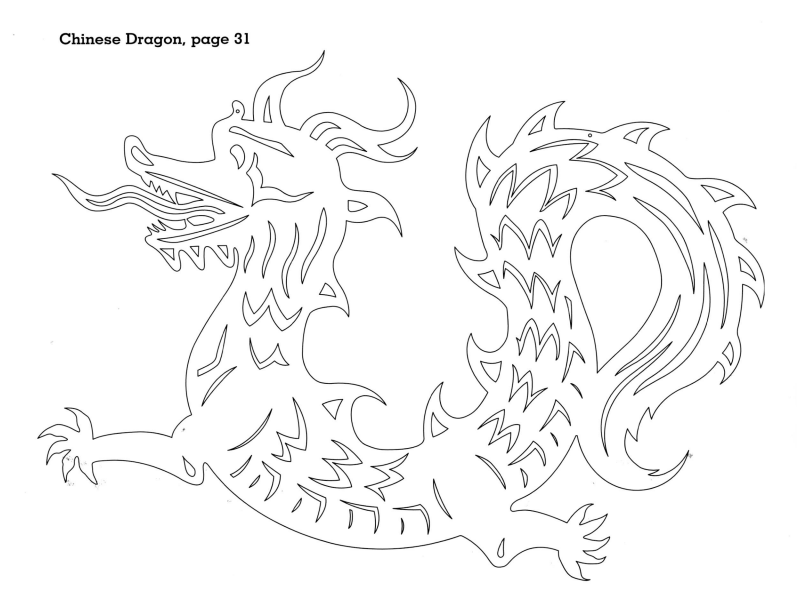

Mosaic Window Hanging, page 35

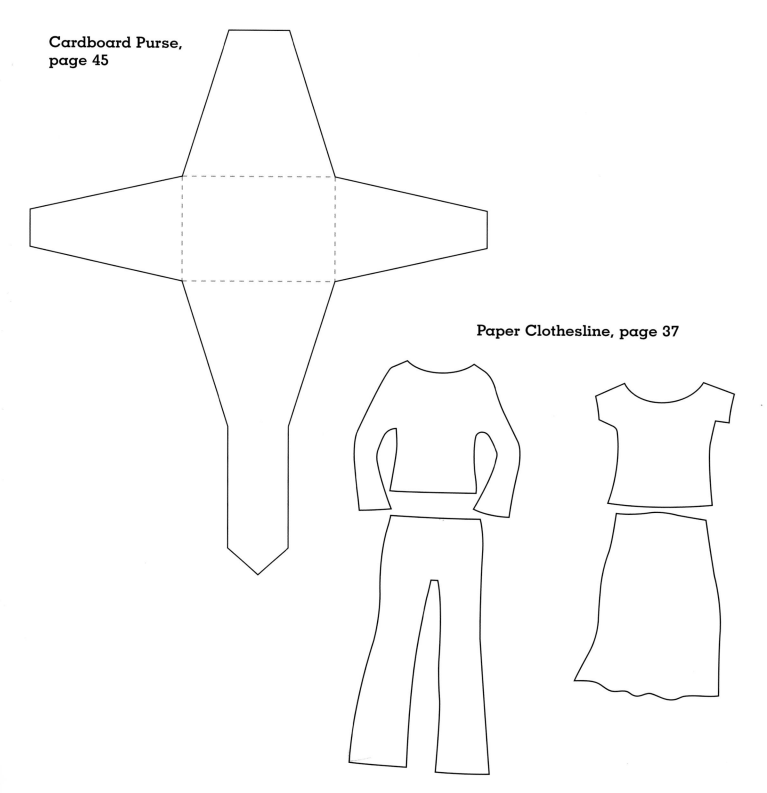

Cardboard Purse, page 45

Paper Clothesline, page 37

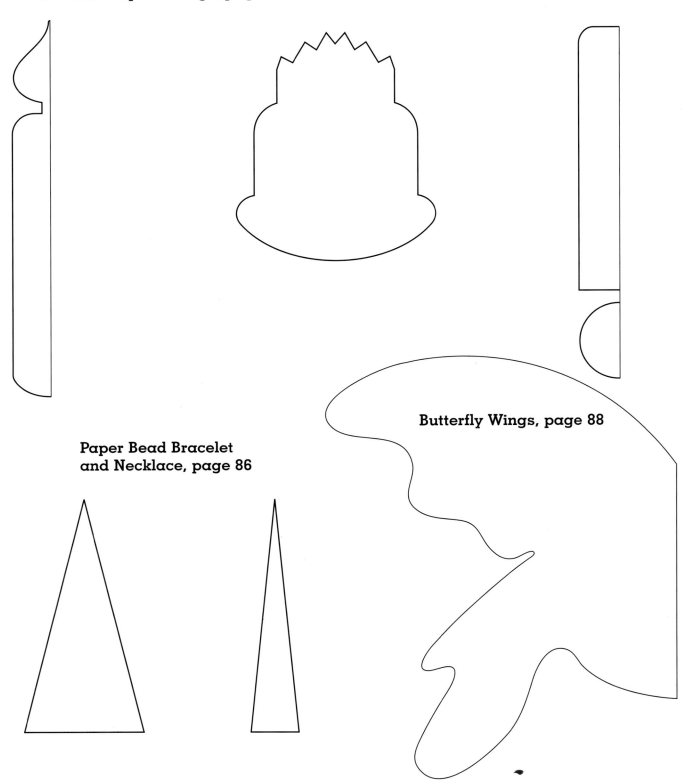

3-D Birthday Greetings, page 56

**Paper Bead Bracelet
and Necklace, page 86**

Butterfly Wings, page 88

Princess Mask, page 98

My Pet Pig, page 102

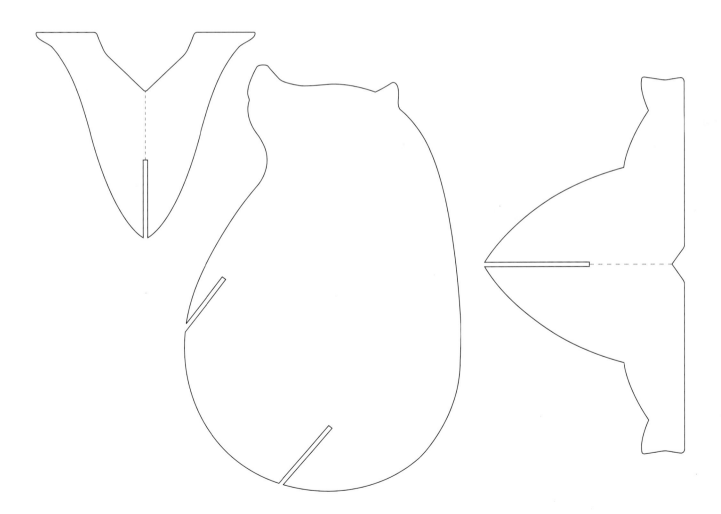

Metric Conversion Chart

¼ inch = 6 mm
½ inch = 1.3 cm
¾ inch = 1.9 cm
1 inch = 2.5 cm
2 inches = 5.1 cm
3 inches = 7.6 cm
4 inches = 10.2 cm
5 inches = 12.7 cm
6 inches = 15 cm
7 inches = 17.5 cm
8 inches = 20 cm
9 inches = 22.5 cm
10 inches = 25 cm
11 inches = 27.5
12 inches = 30 cm
To convert inches to centimeters, multiply by 2.5.

Acknowledgments

Thanks to our wonderful models: **Chance Barry, Karlie Budge, Aja Cobbs, Betty Cobbs, Chloe Heimer, Boone Kaeck, Dorothy Kaeck, Sarah Levinson, Corrinna Matthews, Olivia Patterson, Candace Richardson, Jasmine Villareal, Tobie Grace Weshner, Anna Weshner-Dunning, Chelsea Pryor Wise, John Zimmerman, Lila Zimmerman,** and **Sebastian** (woof!).

Thanks to the big kids at heart who made the projects in this book.

Karen Timm made the 3-D Birthday Greetings on page 56, The Amazing Enveletter on page 58, Wrinkly Gift Wrap on page 65, and Paper Bead Bracelet and Necklace on page 86.

Amy Van Aarle created the Shake-It-Up Journal on page 21, Food Magnets on page 24, Sponge-Painted Photo Album on page 25, Paper Clothesline on page 37, Paper-Filled Ornaments on page 50, and Candy Wrapper Lunch Box on page 92.

Kathryn Temple's projects are the Orizomegami Clipboard on page 19, Dream Travel Box on page 23, Chinese Dragon on page 31, Flower Lights on page 32, Cardboard Purse on page 45, Book Necklace on page 60, Interlocking Paper Bracelet on page 62, Super Stars on page 77, Butterfly Wings on page 88, Rock Box on page 100, My Pet Pig on page 102, and the Tissue Paper Bowl on page 104.

Terry Taylor's Pet Silhouettes appears on page 40.

Ambra Lowenstein made the Mosaic Window Hanging on page 35, Place Mat on page 47, Monster Mask on page 95, and Princess Mask on page 98.

Mary d'Alton's Kirigami Gift Tags appear on page 34.

Marilyn Hastings made the Garland on page 42, Holiday Heart Box on page 44, Paper Bouquet on page 51, Animal Print Box on page 54, Bobble-Head Dog on page 68, Crane Earrings on page 75, and Flying Crane on page 76.

Lynn Krucke created the Stained Glass Candleholder on page 84 and the Floral Box Lid Clock on page 91.

Marthe Le Van's Magnificent Magnets appear on page 85.

And, as always, thanks to the crew at Lark Books, especially **Stacey Budge, Celia Naranjo, Deborah Morgenthal,** and **Paige Gilchrist.**

A Note About Suppliers

Usually, the supplies you need for making the projects in Lark books can be found at your local craft supply store, discount mart, home improvement center, or retail shop relevant to the topic of the book. Occasionally, however, you may need to buy materials or tools from specialty suppliers. In order to provide you with the most up-to-date information, we have created a listing of suppliers on our Web site, which we update on a regular basis. Visit us at www.larkbooks.com, click on "Craft Supply Sources," and then click on the relevant topic. You will find numerous companies listed with their web address and/or mailing address and phone number.